Precipice

The Literary Anthology
of
Write on Edge

Volume II

PRECIPICE COMMITTEE

Editor-in-Chief: Cameron D. Garriepy
Assistant Editor: Angela Amman

Readers:
Angela Amman
Nancy Campbell
Mandy Dawson
Cameron D. Garriepy

STAFF

Managing Editors
Angela Amman, Cameron D. Garriepy
Assistant Editors: Mandy Dawson, Kirsten Piccini,
Roxanne Piskel

Founding Editors: Ericka Clay, Cheryl Rosenberg
Staff Emeritus: Nichole Beaudry, Galit Breen,
Nancy Campbell, Kate Sluiter

ACKNOWLEDGEMENTS

The Editorial Staff would like to thank everyone whose contributions to both The Red Dress Club and Write on Edge have made this collection possible.

We are lucky to have you.

CONTENTS

Heads

Tails

"You never know what worse luck your bad luck has saved you from."

~ Cormac McCarthy, *No Country for Old Men*

HEADS

With My Good Hand
poem by
Marian Kent

Salt over my shoulder means go away!
Your revenge not welcome now I'm older;
in weaker moments, I'd beg you to stay,
       hence, salt over my shoulder.

Before, together, our fissures smoldered,
your heat stoking my molten apogee;
like fire, in time the embers grew colder,

our chinks from burning red reduced to grey.
Now, in green, my wounds are growing bolder
but superstition won't get in the way:
       yes, salt over my shoulder.

Balls

fiction by

Jessie Bishop Powell

Kelly rubbed the bandage on her right leg and winced, wishing she had spare energy to heal the wound. She hated this stretch of 331, where there were no streetlights between the podunk towns, and every reflection might be Kip. For all she knew, every reflection *was* him. He infected everything.

In back, Amber shifted in her carseat and Luna yawned. Then, Luna said, "Mom, stop. He's up there."

"You're sure?"

Luna didn't answer. Kelly didn't know why she had asked.

"How far?" Kelly braked. At this hour, she didn't have to worry about halting traffic. Her beat-up sedan was the only thing on the road.

"Ten, fifteen miles?"

"Is he coming closer?"

"No. Just…sitting there."

Kelly had driven the route enough in her teens and twenties; it hadn't changed in the decade or more since she had last been home. There was a chance to change course in the next little town. "We'll head for Destin instead of Pensacola." She started the car again. But Kip surely knew that too. He had passed them, after all, and if Luna could find her father, then he could find her. He had probably done it much sooner. If he was standing beyond the fork, then he wanted Kelly to take it.

He was tormenting her, herding her away from the haven of her sister's house. But if she diverted, he would have to move to catch her. And anything that delayed him bought Kelly time. If she couldn't get to Jane, she might reach the Gulf. The ocean made powerful magic for a water witch, even one as badly out of practice as herself.

"Mom, I can't sleep." Amber's seat rumbled as she squirmed in it. "These things are making my butt numb."

"What things?"

"Daddy's crystal balls."

"His... Amber did you take your father's...?" Fear emptied Kelly's lungs.

"He was being mean to you."

"You were supposed to go straight to the car! How many—"

Luna interrupted Kelly. "All seven. It looks like she took all seven. I'm sorry. I should have stayed with her instead of banging on doors."

The balls were small; Kip often disguised them as golfballs. But they were powerful talismans, each one a year in the crafting.

"I'm sorry." Amber said.

"No. Good girl." Kelly forced her mind away from thoughts of Amber in Kip's truck, right next to the hellhound. "Good girls. Throw one out, Luna. Roll down your window and toss it hard."

"Do you think he'll follow them?"

"I have to hope so. Their size will make them hard to find in the dark." Surely he thought *she* had taken them. *Don't hold it against the baby. Blame me.* Still, it was an edge she hadn't realized she held. "Chuck one every few miles, but keep the last one. I want to sink it."

She turned at the fork and flexed her fingers on her bandage. For the first time since Birmingham, she hoped they might reach safety.

Roaring barks assaulted Kelly's ears. She screamed, veered, and then accelerated as a monstrous dog jumped out of the ditch. The hellhound kept pace, snapping its jaws.

"Roll up your window. Give me one of those balls." If Kip could draw energy from them, so could she. Even a week ago, she wouldn't have dared to try. Violating Kip's boundaries carried heavy punishment. But, a week ago Kip hadn't backhanded Luna to punish Kelly. A week ago she thought he still might love them, if she could be a better wife and mother. Even yesterday she wouldn't have dared his magic, but everything changed when he shattered the motel windows while they were sleeping.

That memory pursued her with the monster's relentless bark. When he had blasted into the room, wielding a glass shard, Kelly had bellowed and jumped, anything to make him look at her and not their daughters. And look he did. He lunged at

Kelly as Luna shepherded Amber out onto the walkway behind his back.

Kelly dove into the bathroom and the tub she had filled against this possibility. She threw her magic at him in soaking waves, and, when the water was gone, she ran past him out of the room. It had only worked because she caught him off guard. He hadn't expected her to fight back. Didn't think she still had the power. Until she had done it, she hadn't been entirely sure herself. She had cast a stamp on the drenched carpet, a seal he couldn't cross without breaking her spell. It hadn't stopped him, but it slowed him down.

Outside, she found Luna banging on the other guests' doors. "Call 911! My dad's attacking my mom!"

"Baby, I've been telling you for twenty five hundred miles that the police can't do anything to him. Where's your sister?"

"In the car."

It was only when she reached the highway and her adrenaline dropped off that she realized he had cut her leg with the window glass. She rummaged in the glove box for the first aid kit and bandaged herself without stopping. Amber had been the bravest of them all, scuttling into the pickup right beside the monster whose teeth now flashed next to the car.

Kip had as good as caught them. Here in rural Alabama, even if Luna's cell phone hadn't been abandoned on the motel nightstand, there probably wouldn't have been any signal to call Jane. Kelly wished she had used her magic more in the last decade, instead of trying to maintain the semblance of normalcy. She wished she could feel her sister as she had been able to in childhood, the way Luna could feel Kip. She wanted Jane powerfully right now. Instead, she took the ball Luna handed over the seat.

The dog's noise didn't dissipate, though it should have if Luna had raised the window. Indeed, it got louder.

"I told you..." Kelly spared a glance in the rearview mirror. Luna had unbuckled and she now knelt on her seat, her left arm braced against the door frame, the right cocked for pitching.

"Mom, what's the spell?"

"Luna..."

"What's the *spell*?"

Kelly rolled her own ball in her hands. Her grandmother had told her, "The language doesn't matter, but use something you don't normally speak. Or else you'll be hurling magic every time you say good morning."

Kelly gulped. Luna's first lessons weren't supposed to go like this.

"From this I draw my strength. Dari ini saya menarik kekuatan saya." It had been so long since she had spoken those words. So long since she had found power in anything besides water. But the magic was true. Warmth radiated up her arm as she spoke. "Dari ini saya menarik kekuatan saya." She reached out to Luna with her mind and found her daughter reaching back in the same way. "Say it, then throw."

"Dari ini ..."

The dog jumped, jolting the car. Steering with one hand, Kelly returned her eyes to the road. Luna ran the rest of the syllables together into a single word. Through their connected minds, Kelly felt the ball leaving her daughter's fingers and added her own words to the throw. "Membuat tujuan tertentu nya." *Make her aim certain.*

The dog yelped.

"Pegged him!"

"Blood!" Amber screamed.

"Not mine. Give me that box of tissues. It's from Beast."

"Wait, don't wipe it off. Is the dog dead?"

"Mom, this stuff is gross! How should I know?"

"Rub it all over one of those balls and give it to me." Kelly slowed the car to a stop.

"What are you doing, Mom? He's *coming*. Dad is back there!"

"Improvising."

She set aside the ball she had been drawing energy from and took the bloodied one from her older daughter's hand. Amber whimpered. Kelly smeared the blood on her face and shirt, then sent her mind questing. First, she found the dog, still quite alive in the middle of the road. He would be up and after them again soon if Kelly didn't take action. She followed the dog's blood to its master.

Kip was still behind them, closing the distance quickly. He hadn't yet passed by, flying through the fields. Kelly got out of the car. She walked back to Beast, holding the ball in front of her. "Once, we were friends. You used to be half mine." Beast rolled onto his belly and whined. He laid his ears

8

back against his head. "I know. It's been a long time, and you're his dog now. But I need a favor. Do you understand what he sent you to do?" Beast growled. Even a hellhound was only a dog, and this one had orders.

Kelly had reached him now. He wouldn't need much momentum to attack. She held the ball tightly and scooped up the one Luna had thrown, giving herself over to the peculiar ecstasy of a commanding trance. She rubbed the second ball along the oozing gauze on her leg, mixing her blood with Beast's, and with the dirt and asphalt of the road. "Menghidupkan mantra pada tuannya." *Turn the spell on its master.* "I need you to find him, Beast. Bite him for me. Rip out his throat if you can get to it."

Beast staggered to his feet, his skull already healing where Luna had cracked it. He stretched his front legs out long, not a bow or an admission of Kelly's authority, but an acknowledgment. She held his blood. For now, she could compel him. He turned and trotted into the ditch, his vast body vanishing into the foliage.

Kelly shook off the trance and hurried back to the car. That was three of the seven balls she couldn't throw. One imbued with her power, two more with Beast's blood, and one of those filled with Luna's magic. But that still left four. She hoped for nothing as she started again towards the coast.

"Is it a good idea to leave Beast alive?" Luna asked.

"No, but neither is killing him. This way, your father may have to fight through his own magic if he lands."

"But what about Beast?" asked Amber. "Beast loves me."

Kelly didn't answer.

Now that she had homed in on Kip's presence through Beast's blood, she could monitor his progress. He fell behind each time Luna threw a ball, but it was ground he seemed to make up quickly. Finally, Kelly passed onto Destin's Island and skidded to a stop in a resort parking lot. "Luna, take my shirt. Give me yours."

"What?"

"I need to fool his other senses with his eyes. I can cast a glamour that will look like you from above. I need something of yours too, Amber."

"But I want my shirt!" Amber shrank away from Kelly's reaching hands.

"Would her carseat cover work?" Luna was already ripping it loose.

"Probably. Now get under the car."

"Mom, wait! I don't even know what my magic is!"

Kelly stopped stripping off her shirt. Luna didn't want to know about her magic. She wanted to know that Kelly would be back to tell her later. "Air," she said. She pulled her girls into her arms. "You've got his air mastery."

"What about me, Mama? What's my magic?"

Kelly knelt. "I'm beginning to think you have something rare, Amber. I think you have luck."

"Mama, what's going to happen—"

Kelly pulled them into another embrace to drown out Amber's question. "Keep Amber under the car," she said. "When he passes over, when he's completely gone, run into the resort."

"What do I say?"

"The same thing you did at the motel. Your dad is attacking your mom. Take this." It was the ball already imbued with Luna's magic. "Keep it close. My compulsion will keep Beast away, if he was ever really after *you*. Call Aunt Jane as soon as you can. She will shelter you in Pensacola."

Then she took one ball and Luna's shirt in her left hand, and the other ball and Amber's carseat cover in her right and ran down the beach. She heard the beat of Kip's wings long before her feet touched the surf, and she picked up her pace. She risked a glance over her shoulder to see him pass over the car without pause. His body blotted out the night's sliver of moon. Good. He was coming for her, leaving them. Beast erupted from the sand dunes to her left. She ran for the water.

Beast reached her and slowed to match her pace. Whether he was protecting or hunting her, Kelly could not say. Finally, the sand grew wet, and then her feet splashed into the shallows. Now, she dropped the glamour, letting the shirt and carseat cover go. Above her, Kip screamed his night bird fury.

Kelly jammed the balls into her bra and stripped naked to the waist. Beast followed her into the water, plunging into the waves as if he weren't born of fire. As Kelly retrieved the balls, a net descended over her head. Oh, Kip had prepared well. She threw herself forward, tried to dive. But the water was too shallow, and the net pulled taut.

And *then* Beast attacked. He threw his soaking body over Kelly's, forcing her down in spite of the tangling fabric. An instant later, she was free. She surfaced to see the dog flying up, trapped in her place.

She let the balls go. She didn't need them now. She leapt and seized the net's last dangling fibers. Kip lurched. Kelly touched down again, and she swam forward, calling to the ocean to hold her. The water clung to her, whispering its hidden topography.

Beast tumbled loose and knocked her under, but she held tight. And then she reached the drop off. Finally, she could dive. Without releasing the webbing, Kelly plunged her head beneath the waves, dragging her husband with her.

He let go.

No matter. He was committed to hunting her. The girls were safe. She swam with swift, sure strokes, calling on the strength of her mother and her grandmother. She pulled her legs together, and she did not need words to cast this spell. It had always come without effort, this fusing of skin and muscle, this growth of scales.

She threw herself skyward, tempting Kip, taunting him as her ancestors had taunted sailors for so many generations. She dove again, reached the ocean floor too quickly and shot up once more into the air. "Come for me!" She called him, as she had done years ago, when their magic had been a current of desire. "Catch me!"

She laughed and dove. It took longer to reach the bottom now, and the temperature dropped off like the crust of the earth. She thrust up, this time using her tail's power to carry her high. Kip dropped and swiped at her with his bird's talons, a clumsy maneuver that still brought him in range. She seized his claws and, although they sliced her hands, she squeezed. Her momentum dragged them down, and for the first time in longer than she could count, *she* had control. Kip splashed atop her, a huge black eagle who had never been able to swim. Kelly released him. The saltwater stung her bleeding hands, and she called on the pain for strength.

And there was Beast again. The dog seized one of its master's wings in its massive jaws. Kip thrashed in the Gulf of Mexico. Kelly splashed on top of the eagle, wrapped her arms around his wings and forced all three of them underwater. She slapped the surface with her tail one last time as she dragged them down.

Beast dove with her, pulling Kip impossibly deep before he released the wing and kicked off Kelly's back to paddle for the surface. The eagle struggled and twisted, his desperation for life and air strong. But he weakened quickly and lost his eagle's body. Slowly, Kip returned to his own shape. Now Kelly embraced the soft arms that had once cradled her, the hands that had slashed her earlier. She held him under as his heart stilled. At last, she let him go. She kissed his dead mouth one last time before she pushed away. "You loved me once," she told him, "and once, I loved you back."

She surfaced amid pools of light cast by helicopters and search boats. Luna had done her job well. Even in his night eagle form, Kip would have been hard pressed to take down all of these to reach his errant wife. Kelly released her tail, allowing her legs to reform. Then, she recognized Beast struggling against the tide.

She considered leaving him. It was impossible to predict what he would do now that he had fulfilled Kelly's command. Besides, the dog was far from his element and nearly spent. It would have been easy to release this last connection to Kip. But, compulsion or no, he had saved her life. And she could hear the echoes of Amber's whisper. "Beast loves me." So she swam towards the dog even as she murmured to the searchers' lights that she was here.

Onboard a Coast Guard ship, wrapped in a thick blanket, she listened to a sailor droning about her good fortune to be found so far from land. "Why do you think he chased you into the ocean? Was he drunk?" His musings seemed more directed towards himself than Kelly. "You must have gotten caught in the rip. Lucky you didn't drown."

"Beast saved me."

The young man nodded and eyed the enormous animal whose head rested on Kelly's shoulder. "Can't nothing beat a loyal dog."

Kelly ran her fingers through Beast's soaking fur. "No," she said. "Nothing." *And*, she reminded herself, *even a hellhound is only a dog.*

Birthday Party
fiction by
Stacey Meservy

I lay in bed staring at the glow of the clock, wondering when 5:30 a.m. had become the time my body decided was morning. It was my birthday—my 90th if I wanted to be precise; which most of the time I didn't.

I sat up slowly, everything moved like molasses anymore, and stretched my legs. These bones might have been 90, but my heart and soul were still somewhere in my early thirties.

I closed my eyes and let the memories of my life drift through my mind, like so many waves in the sea. I could remember the births of my children as if they were yesterday. I could hear their giggles and smell their sweet fresh-from-the-bath smell. I could see my husband standing at the bathroom sink, even though he had been gone for ten long years.

I still missed him every single day.

My husband wasn't my first love. No. He was my longest love and my companion for 55 years, but I loved another first.

I leaned over and opened the bottom drawer of my nightstand and pulled out my worn photo album. It had become tradition on my birthday, after my husband passed, to look through the album and remember my life. I glanced through yellowed pictures of beaming babies and graduations, but soon turned to the back of the album and slipped out the picture I was looking for. It was the only one I had of him. His youth forever memorialized in the faded photograph still made me smile.

We met on my 18th birthday. It was a warm summer day and the smell of lilacs hung heavy in the air. My mother had decorated the backyard in pink ribbon; soft pink tablecloths donned the tables. She spent months preparing and surprised me by inviting my friends and family.

My cousin's date turned out to be my first love, a sin I would never apologize for.

I remembered the moment he walked into my backyard. His smile was contagious and lit up his blue eyes. He was vibrant, full of life and we became fast friends that night. As the sun set on my birthday, we sat huddled together on the backyard bench giggling and talking well past curfew.

The stars sparkled in a way they never had before. He pointed out constellations and gave them names. I can still pick out most of them on a clear night.

I traced the outline of the face in the faded photograph. With my eyes closed, I was 18 again and full of life with a world of possibilities laid out before me.

The next weekend, he had invited me to go dancing. I was so nervous; I spent the day in tears because my hair wouldn't curl right. The moment I opened the door and he smiled, all of my butterflies flitted away. He offered his arm and we walked to the town hall.

When I tell my children and grandchildren about our courtship, they like to tease me about how it can't have possibly been that good. But it was. He was.

We danced every single dance, laughing and talking and enjoying each other's company. He walked me home and we shared the first of many kisses until my mother flickered the porch light. I blushed, but he simply kissed my hand and asked for another evening.

He courted me for six wonderful months before my father began to ask about wedding plans. He made an appointment to speak to my father about taking my hand in marriage.

As the reality of a life together loomed, a letter arrived that would forever change our future. He was drafted into the Army. He didn't have any real skill or ability to provide a home for me or a future family, and the Army seemed like the best way to ensure a future, even if it wasn't a choice he willingly made.

He promised he would come back and marry me, but it was a promise he couldn't keep.

My aged fingers continued tracing his beautiful face as I remembered the moment this picture symbolized. He was dressed in his uniform with his bag slung over his back and a twinkle in his eye. He kissed my tears away and told me to make use of the camera I was holding.

I stood back and with a wink he told me he loved me as I snapped the picture. I watched him board the vessel that sent him to his death, with hope in my heart and a simple gold promise ring around my finger. I waved my hanky as the boat pulled away from the dock.

A tear rolled down my cheek as I recalled the day his mother told me the news, that moment forever etched in my mind. I wept that day and left my heart in a million shattered pieces by the phone. I wouldn't be able to collect them again for many years to come.

I dried my tears and ran a hand through my silver hair and felt for the gold band still tucked away in the top drawer, the only tangible thing I had left of him. I had stopped wondering *what if* so many years ago. I had led a full and busy life, and was grateful for every moment. In a few hours' time, my children, grandchildren and great-grandchildren would gather for a party.

It's not every day a gal turns 90.

I slipped the smiling face back in its place, pushing those memories aside and finished looking through the album. I paused on my wedding picture and traced the face of the man who shared my life with me. A smile spread through my soul.

It had been a good life. I had been so lucky to find the pieces of my heart again. Our courtship had been so different from the whirlwind of my first love. He had handed me the pieces one at a time and waited until I was ready.

After I buried the love of my life, I also buried myself in my education and became a grade school teacher. I greeted my 4th graders with a broken smile each day, forgetting my pain by burying myself in their futures.

I had resigned myself to becoming an old maid, but my 21st birthday changed my mind. My mother, once again throwing me one of her epic parties, threw this one with one thing in mind: to find me a spouse. I was bitter and angry. I spent the evening hiding on the bench where I had spent my 18th birthday, only this time in tears and frustration.

The man I would marry approached me and, without asking, took a seat next to me. I asked him to leave and he ignored me, his stubborn streak showing early, but would also prove to be my saving grace. We sat in silence for half an hour and when the stars began to twinkle, he asked me if I knew any of the constellations.

My bitter laugh wasn't off-putting enough and as I began to point out the ones I knew, his eyes smiled with kindness. I let my guard down and we had a pleasant conversation, but one I was happy to forget as soon as it was over.

He stopped by my house every night for two weeks to ask me if I would go to dinner. When I finally agreed, I let him know it was only out of pity and so he would stop asking. He smiled and said that was just fine with him.

We had dinner on the pier, and that was the first time I really looked at him. He was only three inches taller than me. He had dirty brown hair and dull eyes. But he had a gentle face and a patient manner. He was handsome in a way that I would come to love and trust.

We walked along the beach and watched the sun set. He stood next to me on the beach allowing for the space to exist between us, then walked me home. I was afraid he would try to kiss me at the door, but he somehow knew not to try. He simply shook my hand, thanked me for a lovely evening and asked if we could have dinner at the same time the following week.

One dinner at a time was how our relationship grew. In time I was able to laugh and hold his hand. Our first kiss was on my 22nd birthday.

It took nearly two years of patient courting before I would consent to marriage, and even then, I'm not sure I was convinced that I loved him. But he loved me and, in the end, that was what I needed.

We built a life together and his patience allowed me time to heal and, in time, to love him back.

Our home was filled with so much love in the end. Three children would run through our hallways, their laughter still echoed in my mind when I walked through my home. His voice boomed through the front door as he returned home every night, and the children ran to greet their father. He would hug each of them, and then kiss me.

My eyes wrinkled a smile as I thought of sending our children off to college, watching them drive away from our front porch as my husband and I stood hand in hand. Age began to show on each of us. We moved slower and ached more. The "what ifs" came less often as we grew older and the memory of my lost love faded with time and the vibrancy of life took over.

My husband died from a sudden heart attack. One day we were walking together, watching the sun set, and a few short days later, I stood at his graveside. I was happy that he hadn't suffered, but angry that I had no warning. I was a widow and it brought back the old feelings.

Tears came freely as I remembered that dark time. It was a time that would be short-lived as the evidence of our happiness surrounded me. My grandchildren visited often and I watched as their children toddled about causing their parents undue stress. My family was a constant reminder of the life I had lived with an amazing man, a man I had been lucky enough to meet.

I closed the album and returned it to its place in the drawer. It was time to get moving. My guests would arrive before I knew it and I wanted to make sure these old bones were ready for the party of a lifetime.

Heads or Tails?

memoir by

Morgan Kellum

Amongst our circle of friends, it's all anyone is talking about. It's impossible to cross campus, answer the phone, or walk through the University Center without somebody asking, "Are you going?"

And, worse yet, they might inquire about who you asked.

"I think we're up to fifteen couples," exclaims the instigator of this crazy plan that has my stomach tied in knots. "That means there will be at least thirty of us all going together! It's so exciting! Who did you ask? I need to know this week so I can get the tickets. Of course, remember to keep our destination a secret...only the girls are supposed to know where we're going."

My stomach drops to somewhere around my knees and I feel my jaw locking up, a forced smile spreads across my face, tense and fake. "Uh, right. I haven't asked anyone yet. But I will. I just have to check with Deb." Shifting my backpack to my left shoulder, I bail on a real answer, skirting the truth. I've worked hard to keep my crush a secret, motivated by the horrifying prospect of being found out or turned down and I feel my knees turn to jelly. "I'll talk to you later," I say as I make my escape, ducking into the office where I work, seeking safety in seclusion and paperwork.

In the midst of filing a three-foot pile of duplicates, I hear a tap on the window. Glancing up, my stomach does a different flip-flop. A roller coaster drop, thrilling, seizing my breath and making my heart rise to my throat. He smiles through the window and waves. I muster a smile that I hope is enchanting and return his wave, willing myself to beckon him in. I could ask him now in the hustle and bustle between classes and that way if he says "no," he can hurry away and I can save face.

Just get it over with and then you can move on, I plead. *You never know, he might accept*, I think. *Who ever thought this group date would be fun?* I grumble.

But instead, I just wave and smile and watch him adjust his messenger bag and saunter away. Maybe later. *But not too much later. He's bound to be snatched up*, I remind myself. A fresh wave of anxiety washes over me as I yank open the metal filing cabinet and set back to work.

"Tonight's the night!" Deb announces. "We have to ask someone now or we'll be the only ones staying home." I chew on my lip and nod, praying for just a smidgen of bravery to at least tell my best friend about my crush. "How about Brett and Tim? We could ask them. They're friends, and we're friends so that would be fun. What do you think?"

Could it be that easy? I remember Brett's smiling face framed in the office window, his blue-green eyes and curly hair; I remind myself to breathe. What if I let Deb do the asking and, just by luck, Brett and I could be partnered up with no risk on my part? I have a fifty-fifty chance this will work out.

For the first time since this group date was concocted, I feel my stomach unknot. "Sure," I say with a shrug, feigning a tranquility that is only skin deep. Under my nonchalant veneer, my heart pounds.

"But I bet we'd each have to pick one," Deb sighs. Cocking her head to the left, she asks, "Who do you want to go with?"

In that heartbeat, my peace evaporates. "Uh...well..." *Why can't you just say his name? Just say, "Brett." That's it. This is Deb you are talking to. She'll be thrilled!* I take a deep breath, steel myself against the inevitable teasing and open my mouth to respond.

But then Deb laughs, oblivious to my inner turmoil. "I guess we could always just flip a coin to see who you go with. I don't really have a preference." With an amazing degree of cowardice, I nod, unable to stir up enough courage to just speak his name. I watch silently as Deb digs around in her purse for a penny. I toss up a little popcorn prayer in case God is concerned with the insignificant heart issues of a love-sick college girl, and I swallow hard.

"Here we go! Heads for Brett and tails for Tim?" Deb asks, looking at me, unaware of my trembling hands and heart palpitations.

"Um...great." Wide-eyed I watch the copper coin fly into the air, flip several times, and fall to the floor. After a bounce and roll, the penny spins a few times and stops.

Heads.

Relief washes over me as I stare at Lincoln's profile, happiness mixed with a smidgen of guilt for being too weak to admit my affections. Maybe I had just enough luck to secure this one date. Or maybe that prayer was sufficient. Regardless, I smile as Deb dials the number for the house the guys share. Smashing our cheeks together, in tandem we ask them out on the group date and, though we fail to designate who is asking who, we hang up with giggles and smiles. An exhilarating sense of liberation from these haunting fears of rejection washes over me and I'm flooded with relief.

The weeks pass and the date is a success. Dinner is fun, the circus is entertaining, and I'm pleasantly surprised to find Brett gravitating toward me. In the coming months, we find ourselves falling into a comfortable routine of coffee shop dates and walks around campus Before I know it, I, with my overly-cautious optimism, am thrilled to call us a couple.

During a chilly walk, my hand tucked into the crook of his arm, our proximity keeping one-half of each of us warm, the conversation floats back to that first date. "You know," he smirks, "when you called with your invitation, you never made it exactly clear who you wanted to take to the circus." I shrug, grateful for the star-filled night to hide my blush. "But I told Tim as soon as you hung up that I wanted you." My cheeks burn and I feel plenty toasty now, a goofy grin spreading across my face, unseen in the dark.

Fast forward 18 years.

Brett pats the cushion next to him on the couch, cocks his head and smiles. His face has a few more lines and his hair is buzzed short, but those same blue-green eyes search my face. I grin and sigh, settling my tired body into the crook of his arm, relieved that it's bedtime and all four kids are down for the night. Pulling the afghan over my lap, he gives me a squeeze and then flips through Netflix, looking for one of our shows. "I think we need something to make us laugh. I love to hear you laugh." I feel my eyes tear up a bit as he leans in for a kiss.

I can't help but be in awe that this man sitting by my side loves me. My brain has trouble accepting this truth, especially on those days when I feel rather unlovable. Or on nights like tonight when the day was long and the bedtime routine excruciatingly longer, and I'm grumpy. He loves me, and he has a for a long time, and I believe he will love me for a longer time still. What a gift! What a wonder! What a stroke of... luck?

No. Not luck. In my little life, with my limited eyesight, that small flip of a coin could appear to be the great catalyst for this partnership, this enduring romance, this family of six. But it's not. It's not luck —it's love. Not our heart-pattering, palm-sweating, nerve-wracking, immature, teenage love, mind you, but God's enduring love. Before I knew that I would need a steady, patient, generous, servant-hearted man to share my life's adventures with, God had orchestrated our first date. And He has continued to choreograph every one of the 6,574 days since that trip to the circus.

I lean my head against his shoulder and feel today's circus-like craziness ease out of me as we laugh along with Liz Lemon and Jenna on *30 Rock*. And then we hear something. A squeak from upstairs; a little voice calling through the railing about a pokey toenail. Brett pauses our show and turns to me. "Rock, Paper, Scissors?"

Maybe I'll get lucky again.

The Pendant

fiction by

Roxanne Piskel

Akira's grandmother was born and raised in a small town several hours outside of Tokyo. She came to America a few years after Akira was born, and only because she believed she might overwise never see her grandchild. She never adjusted to life in America, often spending her evenings grumbling in Japanese to Akira's mother – her daughter – about how none of the silly white children Akira befriended knew how to respect their elders.

She was a strong woman who yielded only to her husband, a man who died from cancer a year before Akira's grandmother immigrated to America. She was strict with her children – a son and a daughter – and with her granddaughter. And still, somehow, she spoiled little Akira with an abundance of knowledge and an appreciation for her culture that Akira's parents had never instilled. Our apartment still shows that appreciation, with Akira's collection of *kimonos* she inherited from her grandmother, the traditional tea set that is displayed on a shelf in the living room with a painting of the cherry blossoms blooming in Hiroshima. Our bedroom hosts a bamboo *shoji* in the far corner, the *washi* decorated with delicate depictions of mountainsides and flowers in bloom.

Before she passed away, Akira's grandmother gave her a small pendant on a thin chain. Fearing its loss, she kept it tucked away in a jewelry box until one day, a year after the old woman had died, she decided to finally wear it.

We came home from a quiet dinner party that night and Akira found the broken chain hanging around her neck. The pendant was gone, and there was no way of telling when the chain had snapped. Our friends checked their house; we checked our house as throughly as we could, and I called the cab company. It was nowhere to be found. Akira was heartbroken.

The pendant had been missing for three years, until yesterday when I was cleaning the living room and I found a small metal Japanese *kanji* under a couch cushion. A small ring hung from the top, as if it had once been attached to a necklace of sorts. Akira had just started a new medication that made her physically exhausted all day long. Since she was resting in our bedroom, I decided not to disturb her. I tucked it in my pocket and finished dusting the shelves.

When we were getting ready for bed that night, after dinner, I was emptying my pockets and found the little pendant. I held my palm out to Akira and told her to look at what I had found while cleaning.

Tears sprang from her eyes as she took the pendant and clutched it to her chest.

"It's hers. It's hers." She kept whispering as she wrapped her arms around me and held me tight against her thin and failing body. "Thank you, my love. Thank you."

We crawled into bed after she tucked the pendant safely into the jewelry box on the nightstand. She curled under my arm, her head fitting in the crook like the missing piece in the puzzle that is my body. She sang a Japanese lullaby I recognized as the one she told me her grandmother used to sing to her. When she had finished and we both stared at the dark ceiling, a car outside momentarily splashed light across the textured material and then the room was cast into darkness once again. Our legs twisted together beneath the cool sheet, entwining ourselves together until I didn't know where I ended and she began.

"What does it mean?" I asked her, whispering into the dark.

She responded with a voice filled with sleep as if she were responding from within a dream.

"My love."

Upgrade

fiction by

A. Duffy Batzer

In his opinion, Lucky had been inappropriately named by overly optimistic parents. There wasn't a more auspicious name than Lucky among the leprechauns. It was their bread and butter after all. But the name had never proven to be a boon for him.

Case in point, he had drawn guard duty the day after his best mate's stag do. So while he should have still been unconscious, dreaming of the lovely cleavage of the friendly barmaid and blissfully unaware that half of his face was stuck to the bar floor, he was, instead, conscious and extremely aware of the unfortunate state of his left cheek.

Lucky contemplated just closing his eyes again and trying to ignore the buzzing in his head, but the hangover was not large enough to overcome what would eventually sound like the bells of St. Patrick's if he didn't obey. He peeled his skin from the floor and made it to his hands and knees. He stayed that way for a moment, waiting to see if the room would slow down enough to make a try at standing, and if his stomach was going to add to the sticky potential of the floor. Eventually everything stayed in its place, and his stomach remembered it had an iron lining.

Lucky stood. Lucky swayed. Lucky belched. With the help of a bar stool, he managed to stay standing. Working his way down the line of bar stools, he headed toward the door. On his way he had to step over several of his party companions, including Clem—the groom-to-be—who, Lucky noticed with a glower, had his head pillowed on the spectacular bosom of the barmaid. With a sigh, he yanked his green top hat from the stand by the door and pushed out into the day.

And, oh, what a bright and cheery day it was; one that made Lucky groan and pull his ridiculous shamrock bedecked hat further down over his eyes. He prayed that the weather on the other side of the rainbow would be one of those days filled with clouds and gloom that often blessed Ireland. Head down, hands in pocket, Lucky shuffled down the street, ignoring the sniffs of disapproval of all the industrious Leprechauns passing him on their way to their very important tasks. He decided to head toward the open meadow at the edge of his little village where he could more easily make a portal to The Other Side without getting in any of his neighbors' way and incurring more of their wrath. The alarm in his head went from a mere ringing to an all-out bong.

"All right, you bleeding sadists; I'm moving, aren't I?" Lucky muttered as he quickened his step as much as the hangover would allow. It really was a war in his head, and no matter who won, Lucky was in for a day of general discomfort.

There are moments in life where small points of interest matter more than they should. People know they should always look both ways before crossing the street. Often the glances are quicker than they should be—often the walker is preoccupied. Most of the time, this is not a big deal. The person makes it across the street safely. But every once in awhile, that carelessness matters a great deal to the walker. It changes his life.

Leprechauns open holes between realities as often as people cross the street. Just like humans, they are fallible beings who are wont to forget that fact and are not always as careful as they ought to be. But, again, fate was usually kind or at least indifferent. They got where they were going unharmed.

Stepping through his portal, Lucky got nailed by a Vespa.

As he cartwheeled down the pavement, his vision blurred from the bright blue sky, the gray of the asphalt and the sunny yellow of the Vespa that was now lying on its side, the rider already working to right it. Lucky came to a stop about twenty feet down the road. His vision did not. When it finally did, he was lying on his back looking up at a sky just as dazzling as the one he had left. Figured.

Suddenly, his field of view was filled with a face. It belonged to a young man, probably in his twenties, with red hair, spiked and mussed from being in a helmet, dark brown eyes set in a round face overwhelmed with large ears. Currently, the almost comical features were set in an expression of concern.

"Holy Mary Mother of God mate, are you OK? I swear you came out of nowhere," he said as he tentatively touched Lucky's shoulder.

Fortunately, Leprechauns were tougher than humans. Well, they were bouncier than humans anyway. Lucky was able to sit up with help from the young man.

"Oh, thank goodness! How are you feeling?" Lucky put his head in his hands. "Oh, no, come on now! Deep breaths! Take it easy. I'm going to call the *gardai*!" The young man went to stand up.

Lucky clung to him and muttered, "No, no. I'm fine. No need for all of that." Holding onto the scooter rider's pant leg, he stood up. He regretted it, but he did stay on his feet. He had to close his eyes for just a moment, and that was when the driver got a good look at him. All three feet, covered from head-to-toe in shamrock green, of Lucky. The young man started to stagger back, but then his eyes went to slits and he tightened his grip on the shoulder of Lucky's jacket. He looked Lucky up and down, taking in the top hat, the curly brownish red hair and beard over a ruddy face, the slight pot belly and, of course, the shamrocks. All the shamrocks.

Something like comprehension started to dawn on the youngster's face. "Wait a second. Wait a bloody second..." he drawled. "What? Are you... are you what I think you are? Am I being put on?" He glanced around as if to find other people lurking and laughing.

Suddenly Lucky realized just what a pickle he was in. He tried to focus enough to talk his way out of it. First he tried to lie. His tongue stuck to the roof of his mouth. Great. The magic was starting to take over. Damn. This was going to take some fast thinking and talking.

He went for reassuring and fatherly. "Oh, lad, what are you on about? I think you got more shaken by our little crash than you let on." He patted the boy on his knee and tried to slip away from him. But the friendly tone did not seem to have the desired effect. Lucky was held fast.

The boy exclaimed, "Ha! You are! You are a for-real, in-the-flesh leprechaun! No way! I owe my gran a whopping huge apology!"

Lucky sighed. "I really think you just hit your head. Hard. Really hard."

"Nice try, little man. But I'm willing to go with this. I can suspend disbelief because, if my dear old gran's story is right, you owe me a pot of gold."

Lucky's first reaction was to bluster. He puffed out his chest in indignation. He stood to his full height and stuck out his chin, trying to look the kid in the eye. And then he deflated. He sagged all the way to the ground and ended up clutching his head as it hung between his knees.

"Fuck," he said.

A broad grin broke across the kid's face. "Ha! It's true! Bloody hell. I'm gonna be rich!" He danced a little jig around Lucky, kicking up puffs of dirt from the road. He had let go of the coat the moment Lucky had bowed down, defeated. When his dance finally stopped, he wiped some sweat off of his forehead and asked, "What happens now?"

Lucky got to his feet. He smacked his hands across the knees of his pants and then across his bottom. With an adjustment to his hat to try and block the godforsaken sun, Lucky turned to the actually lucky son-of-a-bitch. With a sigh, he replied, "Follow me."

He shuffled his feet as he led the guy to the other side of the road, through the bushes and brush into a grove of oaks, old trees with deep roots and long, heavy branches that laced together overhead, making it slightly darker underneath them. *At least that was something*, thought Lucky. He moved through the trees doing his best to weave and doubleback and generally be confusing. The rules didn't say he had to make it easy for the kid. In point of fact, his job now was to make it as hard as possible. The kid kept pace, never saying anything or complaining, though he did seem to be breathing hard. *Heh.*

Finally, Lucky looked around. He wasn't quite sure which way the road was, so he figured the kid couldn't be either. He led him to the tree. Lucky stood on one of the upraised roots and squinted up at the young man. "It's buried under this tree." He pointed to the base.

The kid was puffing with his hands on his knees. He glanced down and then back at Lucky. A little breathy, he asked, "And?"

Lucky put his hands on his hips. "And what?"

"Well, how do you get it out?"

"I don't," Lucky chuckled. "I have to show you where it is. I do not have to dig it up for you."

The kid glared. "That's bloody mean. It's not like I carry a spade all over creation on my Vespa."

"Not. My. Problem."

The guy huffed out a breath and scowled. "Fine. What happens if I have to go find a shovel?"

"I wait."

"Okay. Great. I'll be back." The kid turned in a circle and looked around. He pulled a red handkerchief from his pocket. He patted at his sweaty face, then reached up and tied it on a branch. "Just in case," he said as he also pulled a little box out of his pocket. Lucky tilted his head. The kid tapped what appeared to be buttons on the thing, then he nodded. "I should be back in about an hour or so." He glanced around, touched something else on the box, turned and headed off. He turned back a moment later and asked, "You are not allowed to touch anything or move anything?"

Lucky held up his right hand and said, "I promise." The kid headed off. When Lucky deemed he was out of earshot, he moved to a small pond off to his left. He bent down to splash a little into the air and waved his other hand. The water split into droplets and a rainbow formed. Through it he saw his friend, Clem, still passed out at the bar.

"Clem!" he yelled.

The snoring man just snored more. In fact he snored a little louder.

Lucky cupped his hands around his mouth. "Clem!"

With a snort, Clem cracked a bloodshot eye and slurred, "Lucky?"

"Yeah, mate, look. I need help. I got caught."

Clem woke up. "You serious?"

Lucky nodded dejectedly. "As a priest. But I think I have a loophole. I only have an hour though. I need help."

Clem sighed. "What do you need?"

"Handkerchiefs," Lucky replied.

Lucky was sitting by the side of the road by the time the slightly battered Vespa came sputtering back up. The kid applied the brakes, and used his feet to come to a complete stop. He had rigged a kind of scabbard out of a belt and what appeared to be a tube sock, so a shovel scoop was visible just over his left shoulder. He pushed his ride level with the leprechaun.

"Alright, little man. I'm going to dig my way to rich."

Lucky stood and straightened his jacket. "Let's get this over with." He turned to crash his way back through the brush. The boy followed with even louder crashing.

When they emerged from the weedy hedge, Lucky turned to the kid, trying to hide the smirk that wanted to spread across his face. The kid glanced around and then glowered down at Lucky. "Neat trick," he said.

Lucky shrugged. "I just promised to not touch or move anything. I didn't say anything about adding anything."

Lucky and Clem had spent the hour the kid was gone tying red handkerchiefs to all the trees in the grove. It had taken all of their magic reserves, but it was done. Lucky figured the pot of gold was just as safe as ever. He waited for the boy's tantrum to begin. Lucky was hoping he'd cry.

Instead the kid just sighed and turned back to the trees. He pulled the box with the buttons out of his pocket and went to work tapping again. Something on the box beeped. The kid started into the trees. Lucky narrowed his eyes and started following. He had a bad feeling about this. The boy kept staring at the box and making adjustments to his direction. When he finally stopped, Lucky had trouble breathing. He was standing at the right tree. Lucky opened his mouth. Nothing would come out. The kid undid his shovel and shoved it into the ground, putting all his weight on it. He had thrown the first shovelful over his shoulder, in Lucky's direction, when Lucky finally found his voice.

"How in the hell did you know?"

The kid glanced up, but he kept digging. "Because I am not bloody stupid. I listened to my gran. I know how this works. And it is the twenty-first century, mate."

"What does that mean?"

"It means that there are other ways than a bleeding handkerchief to track something." He stopped digging for a minute and pulled the box out of his pocket. He handed it to Lucky and started digging again.

Lucky looked down at the box. It seemed to be a little black block of glass. Lucky turned it over in his hand. "What is it?"

The boy glanced up in disbelief. "Really? Where have you been? It's a smartphone."

"Huh?"

The kid sighed. "It is an electronic device. I can use it to contact other people, and do a lot of other things, including taking pictures to verify I have the right tree. But, more importantly, it has GPS."

Lucky felt like they were suddenly speaking a different language. "Jay Pay Ess?"

"Gee Pee Ess. It tracks your location, or the location of things. I recorded the location of the tree." More dirt went flying.

Lucky studied the object in his hand. Turned it over and over. It sounded like magic.

Chink!

The kid jerked a little as his shovel touched metal. He immediately fell down to his knees and pushed more dirt out of the hole with his hands. With one last brush of his hand, he uncovered the top of the pot of gold. Its gleam was subdued in the shade of the trees, but there was no questioning the sound the coins made as the kid let them run through his fingers. He laughed hysterically, long and loud.

"I'm going to buy my gran the prettiest Sunday dress I can find!" Instead of trying to pull out the pot, he yanked out a pillowcase he had tucked in his belt and started scooping his fortune into it. He paused a moment to look up at Lucky. His look was a little thoughtful and then he said, "Does this fuck you over a whole lot? Does this leave you dirt poor? I mean, you got other investments?"

Lucky stopped for a minute and looked back at the kid. "It is a significant bit of trouble, yes. But I'll muddle through, thanks." He paused before adding, "I'll tell you what though; we could be more even if you would do me a favor before you leave to spend as much gold as quickly as you can."

"Name it."

Lucky held out the smartphone. "Show me how this works?"

The kid smiled widely. "No problem."

Lucky pulled at the neck of his shirt trying to loosen the bow tie just a little. He leaned back against the bar and took a sip from his whiskey. Despite being the best man at Clem's wedding, Lucky was doing his best to remain unobtrusive. There were enough of his relatives there to make things uncomfortable.

Clem came out of the dining room and slid up to stand next to Lucky. He flipped his finger at the bartender and soon had a whiskey of his own. He said to Lucky, "Hiding?"

"Just a little," Lucky replied.

"How pissed are your parents?"

"Pissed enough."

"I have to say, my best man, you seem to be taking your disgrace much better than I would have ever thought."

Lucky sipped slowly and smiled, "It won't last long."

Clem glanced at him and smiled back. "What do you have up your sleeve?"

From his pocket Lucky pulled the smartphone and handed it to Clem.

Clem's confusion was obvious. "What is it?"

"That," Lucky replied, "controls the eyes of God, my friend. And it is going to make us back the gold I lost, and then some. We're going into business together."

"What kind of business?"

Lucky grinned over another sip of whiskey. "Security."

Kismet's Kiss

fiction by
Kirsten A. Piccini

Violet Webster detested Halloween. Even as a child, she never quite grasped the necessity of such a pandering evening. But her best friend Lila considered Halloween the best holiday of the year; a serendipitous night when anything could, and often did, happen.

If I wanted to dress up, bang on doors and beg for things I'd just continue dating.

Yet here she was, leaning up against the bar in Mario's Tavern in a short plaid skirt and white knee socks with her hair in perky pigtails. All because Lila had placed a small seed of hope in her heart. *"Your luck could change tonight; you never who you're going to meet."*

She placed the small red straw into the corner of her mouth and took a generous sip of her peach schnapps and cranberry while her eyes scanned the dusty dimly lit establishment, trying to pin down the whereabouts of Chad, Lila, and Ryan. She was sure she had seen her best friend's impeccable blonde highlights, but when she looked up again, they were nowhere to be found.

Chances were that Lila was in the bathroom again. Ever since she and Ryan had finally gotten pregnant, *after trying for close to 3 years,* Lila was either peeing or barfing. It was not a good look on the girl who used to define fashion, even when she was dressed in her pajamas.

So if Lila was ridding herself of the hors d'oeuvres they'd just loaded up on in a vain attempt to feed her little human, then Ryan was standing close by the door of the ladies' room and Chad was flirting with every guy in a three-mile radius.

Violet tugged at the skirt, the polyester fabric brushing against her naked thigh causing her to wince.

"Hey, who are you supposed to be?" she heard someone behind her ask.

Rattled by the voice, she sloshed her drink and splashed bright pink stains onto her crisp white shirt.

"Shit!"

"Oh sorry, didn't mean to startle you." Strange hands gripping a napkin crowded her personal space as the liquid sloshed again. Violet juggled the drink and tried to stop the hands from making contact with her boobs.

"Easy," the deep voice chuckled, "I'm not trying to cop a feel. I'm just trying to wipe the stains before they set. "

Violet looked up into brown eyes, deep chocolate pools that made her heart and voice stammer. The eyes were looking almost directly into hers and that made her feel sexy and tall, even though she was barely 5'5 in these 3-inch Mary Janes. She suddenly felt like a supermodel.

"Oh, I'm sorry," she apologized, as she started swatting his hands away but doing such a poor job that soon his hands were in the one place she had been trying to keep them away from. An electric current ran through her, and she was sure that even in this dingy, smoke-filled bar he could see the blush that was climbing up her neck and settling in her cheeks.

She placed the goblet she was holding against her face and looked at him.

"I guess you should move your hands now."

"What if I don't want to?"

"Then you need to propose or agree to a courthouse wedding in the morning."

"Done." He laughed, "Hi, I'm Zach. Zach Becker. And you are…"

"I'm Violet, the Catholic schoolgirl." She plucked at the skirt as if the plaid would give her away.

"Well, hello Violet. It's really nice to meet you."

She took in his khaki pants and button down shirt with sleeves rolled halfway up his arms.

"Umm, you're not dressed as anything."

"You caught me." He said with his hands in the air as if she'd apprehended him. "I was just stopping by on my way home since a friend asked me to drop by."

Violet tilted her head thoughtfully. "You could say you're a Blockbuster employee, although they're as extinct as dinosaurs these days. I mean, truthfully, when is the last time you saw a Blockbuster employee?" She cackled at her own joke until cranberry juice was shooting out her nose.

"Jesus, I'm making a mess of this shirt tonight."

"Looks like it might need a trip to the dry cleaners." Zach said with fake seriousness, his brown eyes twinkling. "Maybe my blue button down and khaki pants should go with to keep it company."

"I don't think my *shirt* would mind that at all."

"Really?" He asked, stepping closer to her.

"Really."

She was suddenly embarrassed at how much she longed for his hands to be where she'd shooed them from only moments ago. Hoping that she smelled of peaches and vanilla, and not sausage rigatoni, she leaned in as his face tilted inches from her own. Closing her eyes, she gave in and waited for the magic.

"Vi! There you are!"

Jolted out of the moment, Zach jerked and crashed into her, sending both of them sailing in slow motion; Violet's drink raining down on them as their tangled bodies hit the hardwood floor with a thump.

"Ouch!" Violet moaned, scrambling to sit up and pull her skirt down over her black lace panties.

She looked up to chide Chad, but not before Zach spied the sexy underwear.

Mortified, she struggled to her feet. "Chad! What the hell are you doing?"

"Attempting to save your sullied reputation, my dear. You were about to kiss a complete stranger!"

Violet blushed the color of her spilled drink. "I was no—"

Chad held up his hand. "I was just trying to rescue your virtue before you did something you might regret."

Winking at her, he turned his attention to Zach, who was slowly pulling himself up with the help of a bar stool.

"So, who's your friend?"

Violet shot him a filthy look. "Chad, this is Zach. Zach, this is my very obnoxious, very meddling, and very gay best friend, Chad."

Chad pretended to look hurt. "I'm not obnoxious."

Zach was futilely trying to brush the sticky red drink from his pants, making even more of a mess, when he reached for Chad's hand and shook it.

"It's nice to meet you Chad."

"Not as nice as it is to meet you, Zach." Chad grimaced at his now sticky hand but did nothing to hide the flirt and banter in his voice.

Violet shook her head. "Sorry Chad, I think he plays for the other team."

Turning to Zach, she added, "It's your loss really; Chad is quite a catch. "

Zach pretended to be interested, "Oh yeah?" He looked at Chad and asked "Does he cook, clean and iron?"

"Well, he makes the best chicken marsala I've every tasted, but that's when he can locate the kitchen in that mess he calls an apartment."

Chad shrugged and reached for a napkin from the bar to wipe his hand. "Nobody's perfect."

"I'm a sucker for a home-cooked meal." Zach offered.

Chad grinned. "Oh don't tease me; I fear you are far too straight for me. I mean, look at you, I bet you even play fantasy football."

Zach puffed his chest. "Part of the champion team, 3 years running."

"Just as I feared."

Violet interrupted the exchange. "Oh Zach, don't let Chad fool you. Sure, he has impeccable fashion sense and an iPod full of show tunes, but he'll kick your ass in any sport—fantasy or otherwise.

"Caught." Chad confessed as all three of them burst into laughter.

Violet started to wonder if Lila had been right about the universe sending her a happy ending for once, when her other best friend stumbled into the circle they had created. Lila was looking even greener under the witch's makeup she had applied earlier. One look at the smeared eyeliner and she knew it was time to find Ryan and get Lila out of here.

Zach stared at Lila, a mix of pity and confusion on his face.

"Hey, do I know you?"

Lila glanced up at him, her tiny frame dwarfed next to him.

"I don't think so…" she said, shaking her head, which caused her to heave and hurriedly place a hand over her mouth.

"Is your friend alright?" Zach asked Violet with such concern that she suddenly wanted everyone else to disappear so they could get back to the part with him leaning down to kiss her.

Instead, Violet helped Lila onto a barstool.

"Yep, she's fine." Then she stopped and added, "Well that's not exactly true; she's five months pregnant and insisted on coming out tonight. This was supposed to be her last hurrah but it seems ginger ale and hot dogs wrapped in crescent rolls didn't agree with her plans."

"I just wanted to be a sexy for Ryan," Lila whimpered. "Before he sees me as nothing more than the mother of his child and parenting sucks up every sexual urge either of us has."

All three of them just stared at her.

Lila offered up a weak smile. "Sorry. Just raging pregnancy hormones. Thank goodness Ryan's used to my melodrama."

On cue, her husband turned the corner and stood in the middle of their growing party.

"Buddy, you made it!" He shouted at Zach, smacking him on the back. "Have you met everyone?"

The group eyed Ryan, their stunned silence asking how he knew their new acquaintance.

"Zach's my boss." He explained, taking a sip of his beer.

Chad choked on his martini, Violet turned a deeper shade of pink, and Lila locked eyes with her best friend mouthing the word "Kismet" before she turned green again and threw up all over Zach's shoes.

Three weeks later, Violet was drowning in paperwork.

Day to day, she loved her job in relocation. When a company was sold or acquired, she was part of the first step for complete strangers starting a new life in a new place and it was satisfying to provide stability in such an unpredictable time.

So days when she was fighting with IT about her network and internet access and chasing down contracts that should have been approved by legal a million years ago made her cranky. Today was one of those days.

The final straw was when she stood up to try to fix a jam on the printer and instead knocked over her Diet Coke. It trickled out of the top of the can, creating a small fizzing pond on her new client files before having the audacity to dribble down onto her favorite black peep toe shoes.

"Son of a bitch." She squealed as it made contact with her cotton candy lacquered big toe.

Taking a deep breath, she reached for the files and started dabbing at them with a napkin.

Disgusted and completely frustrated, she started to clean up her desk, when her phone rang. Hoping it was the help desk she grabbed at it and shouted, "This is Violet Webster."

"Violet Webster, the Catholic school girl?" A voice asked.

"Who is this?"

"You don't remember me?" The voice sulked. "Really? My feelings are hurt. Plus my blue shirt and khaki pants are going to suffer from low self esteem now, not to mention the poor Italian leather shoes I had to throw away."

Violet held the phone and blushed furiously, thankful Zach couldn't see her since she'd given up on ever hearing from him.

"Remember you? Zach, you're a jerk."

"Violet, what are you talking about? I told you I'd call." She could almost see him smiling. "So here I am, calling."

"I called and left a message two weeks ago, Zach."

"Well," he stammered, "I've been busy."

"Is that right?" She shot back in teasing voice. "Wow, I didn't know you were championing world peace or coming close to the cure for cancer."

Zach chuckled. "I like you Violet. You don't put up with my bullshit or let me off the hook, and I find that extremely attractive. Tell you what: if I promise to call more often from now on, will you go out with me?"

Violet hesitated.

She liked Zach, liked him enough to wonder what it would feel like to kiss him, liked him enough to want to ask him about his childhood or cook his favorite foods. She even liked him enough to consider thinking that meeting him might mean the end of the current nightmare she called a love life. But something held her back, her thoughts idling instead picturing a happy ending. She instantly feared that Zach would just turn into another man who left her.

Coming out of her own thoughts, she heard Zach's concerned voice. "Vi? Vi, are you there?"

And that's what did it, his innocent use of her nickname.

"I'm here," she whispered.

"Can I take you out Saturday night?"

"Can we meet at Mario's?" She asked.

"Scene of the crime, huh?"

"Seems appropriate, don't you think?"

"Well, as long as our beverages stay in their glasses, I'm in." Zach said. "How does 7 sound?"

Violet inhaled and closed her eyes.

Sink or swim, it's now or never. C'mon Violet, a little risk never hurt anyone.

"I'd like that."

Suddenly, their voices were spilling over one another.

"Well, great. I'll…"

"…see you then…"

Violet waited for the dial tone that signaled the call had ended and then tapped out another number on the keypad. Happily ignoring the dark pond of Diet Coke still dripping off her desk, she listened to the ringing.

"This is Lila."

Smiling at the sound of her best friend's voice, Violet couldn't contain the joy in her own. "Hey Lile; *guess what.*"

Seven Easters
poem by
Angie Kinghorn

I.
Easter. Pews packed, a cross covered in wildflowers.
Voices raised in joy, reaching for harmony.
White, hats, ribbons, lilies,
and blood,
as two lives burrow into the pillowy softness
        of their first home.
They wait in the dark, together
a secret born in the midst of music
        and soaring columns of stone,
stained glass and the hush of holiness.

II.
She waits, cheeks flushed with life and nerves.
More blood after Easter; would this be her
        Good Friday?
No, not her Good Friday. Her day of plenty.
        Of good fortune.
She cries, smiles, cries; shows him the pictures;
        not one but *two*, each in a bubble.
He is frozen; she sees fear in his trembling hands.

They pray, begging God to let them keep
        the gifts he has given;
caressing her belly as if the sleepers can feel
        their love
through layers of flesh and womb.

III.
Sharp smells in the hospital keep her awake
        all night, listening to the rapid
swoosh-swoosh of heartbeats.
Her belly hardens, tightens, she wills it to stop,
        begs God to help her keep these lives safe.
God answers with a nurse bearing a syringe,
        sends her home with more.
Each day, day after eternal day,
she stays...still...on her left side.
Hands over her belly, she feels movement
        inside and out as they slip around like fish.
Please...you're safe here. Stay here.

IV.
The curve of her belly disappears, stretched
        with knees and elbows and heads, forming
corners; sharp, unyielding.
Tears well unbidden as they move
        and battle for space
and she prays for it to end; doubting her strength.
He sits with her, holds her hand,
        swollen out of her ring
watching her belly.
Undulating, changing shape
bruising from the inside.

V.

It is decreed: her body can take no more.
 So it is shaved, filled with tubes, tied down,
 and cut open while she is awake
and cold; so very cold.
He sits at her head and talks, (as if he could distract
her from the uprooting) as the first
is pulled from her.
And then the second, more deeply entrenched,
 wants to stay,
and they push and struggle to pull this second one
 from her.
Then it is done; they are here.

VI.

They are here in the cold, in bright lights. *Nooooooo,*
 they howl.
She is on fire, her insides turning out.
They are safe. They are here.
Where are the pink-tinged clouds of joy?
She should feel lucky; a fierce gratitude.
Instead she is numb; beautifully and utterly numb.
Except for her body—
a shell of exquisite pain.

VII.

What did silence sound like?
What was life *before*?
She walks, rocks, pats, prays for the crying to stop.
Her tears flow along with theirs.
Broken. She is broken; sewn together,
 but not where she's torn.
He knows it;

she knows it;
together, they ask for help.

VIII.
Brokenness does not suit her; she curses her luck,
       her weakness.
Shame drags her beneath the water
       into a death roll.
The pills and deep breathing fight off
       the darkest demons.
She reminds herself it could have been
       so. much. worse.
The nightly news reminds her
it could have been so. much. worse.
The good fortune isn't hers alone;
she includes it in her prayers,
       thanking God every day.

IX.
Seven Easters later, four of them sit
together, in a different pew.
They burrow into her, one on each side.
       She holds them tight.
Kneeling for communion, she watches as
       they are blessed
and thanks God for the blessing.
She is still broken,
but light—and grace—have found their way
       through the cracks,
bringing peace.

The Soldier's Gambit

fiction by

Shelton Keys Dunning

The battle raged far afield, but was still close enough to shake the timbers of the abandoned mill with each fired trebuchet. Tattered sails harnessed what wind they could to grind the grain of ghosts long departed, while the nearby dying waited harvesting by the agents of their gods.

The world was lost, the Omen-Readers whispered.

Cavimi laughed as he propped himself up against the crumbling exterior of the mill. What did Omen-Readers know? They corralled themselves atop mountains and smoked wisp and sage until their eyes bled from their sockets, chanting nonsense to kings for coin. And those fools swallowed every lie.

Blood soaked his tabard, but it wasn't his. He wasn't the type to stick around when he was on the losing side of a conflict. If he was lucky, he wouldn't be missed until nightfall. Vultures began to circle in the distance, summoning another fit of laughter. Luck. Omens. If he wasn't careful, he'd be chanting gibberish on top a mountain. "Not me, not today, thank the gods."

Still, Omen-Readers' words sometimes carried truths, and in this battle were traces of a lost world, a world gone mad with greed and grief. Cavimi withdrew his water-skin and drank its contents with more moderation than his thirst wanted him to. He stoppered the skin and surveyed the bloodied kingdom. The fortress withstood the barrage for a consecutive fourteen days and gave no indication of weakness. He wondered if it was a mirage. He wondered if those within the fortress knew of the hundreds that lay in waste outside the portcullis. He wondered why he wondered.

A peculiar sound, different from the squeaky sails and the grinding stone, resonated from within the mill. Cavimi leapt to his feet, drawing his dagger, and prepared for an ambush that never came. A pair of maidens emerged from the doorways, rushed and crying. "Whoa, where did you come from?"

The ladies froze. "Don't hurt us!" One begged, falling to her knees.

Cavimi looked at the dagger in his hand and hastily re-sheathed it. "Forgive me, *belladonnas*. I was not expecting company."

The beggar remained on her knees, heaving sloppy sobs and tears. The other stiffened despite his show of peace and regarded him with horrified suspicion. "You wear the tabard of Valtirissi."

"Ah, don't let that bother you. I quit the field."

Her eyes narrowed. "You're a traitor?"

He laughed. "I'm sure Countessa di Valtirissi will label me such, but I never swore an oath to her or her armies."

"To whom do you proclaim your loyalty?"

"Why, to myself, my lady." He bowed. "Cavimi Astimio, at your service."

"If you are at my service, then you will help us get to the Bonne."

"I do not work for the nameless or the poor." Cavimi stumbled back to his pitch. "But I wish you great fortune."

"My name is Artesia DiPaccia."

"—Or the *poor.*"

The beggar crawled, staining her knees green. "Please Monsignor. Show us mercy."

Cavimi sized up the beggar. The threads of her garment were fine, but aged, and her *shoon* were sensible. She, the servant, the other, Artesia, was hard to determine. "No name, no method of payment, no deal."

Artesia looked to the castle and back again. "Monsignor, *I am* your payment. You will escort my companion to Bonne. Refuse me again, and you are thrice cursed."

"Bah, I do not believe in curses, and you as my payment?" He pondered this for a long while. "And if I agree to those terms? What is it you expect I shall do with you?"

She didn't blush or flinch. "I expect you shall do as you like with me. Once we get the girl to Bonne."

The beggar protested. Cavimi waved her away. "*Belladonna* Artesia, what if I choose to sell you as a slave? What if I choose to keep you to wife?"

Still, she didn't blush or flinch. "Once we get the girl to Bonne, if either is your wish, I will do as you ask. Do we have an accord?"

"I will need to know your companion's name as well."

"Belladonna is sufficient for the task." Artesia raised up her companion and wiped tears from her delicate cheeks.

"Well then," Cavimi rose again. "The payment is unusual, but you have earned my curiosity and so, therefore, I pledge to see you and your companion to Bonne, where I agree to take possession of said payment."

Artesia nodded. "You shall not have any portion of the payment before, or your entire payment will be forfeit."

Cavimi shrugged. "As you command. Now, time to assume a new identity."

They scavenged the miller's house, finding trouse for the beggar, a cloak for Artesia, and a plain tunic suitable for Cavimi. He shed his Valtirissi colors, turned the tabard inside out, and draped it about the beggar's shoulders. She in turn traded her skirts for the trouse. Artesia took the skirts and tied a knot in the waist. They dumped what they could scavenge in the skirts and secured the hem. Artesia strapped the makeshift travel sack to her back without complaint and they soon departed.

The trek off of the hill along the King's Highway was taken in silence, save for the beggar's random fits of crying. Cavimi thought of his bargain. What would he do with Artesia? She proved herself resourceful; first by masterfully negotiating the terms of their accord, second by the manner in which she repurposed items from the miller's house. And third, as they journeyed on, was the vegetation she gathered. Dandelions and brambleberries, watercress and wild fennel; no edible treat was overlooked. Yes, Artesia was useful.

When they camped the first night, Artesia prepared a meal that satiated them all. They suffered under a cold camp, no lit fire for warmth, for they were still too close to the battle that waged and could be discovered by an ambitious scout. The girls huddled together under Artesia's cloak, and as Cavimi took ground opposite them, he noticed a metallic glint from Artesia's hand. *She slept with a dagger at the ready.* He did the same.

The second day was also spent traveling along the King's Highway in blissful silence. Cavimi whistled some as the sun leached the frosty evening from their skin. He knew this stretch of highway well enough, for he had served out a contract in a little hamlet not far to the east. A twinge of wistful memory drifted to his senses, of the innkeeper's daughter, so fair of face, who captured his desires during his tenure there. In truth, he had not set out to seduce her, and in every respect it was she who instigated the affair. Cavimi wondered if the girl, whose name escaped him, pined away for his return.

Surely not. Years came and went by the decades since he last spoke with her.

"Monsignor, the road!" Belladonna raised a trembling hand to her mouth.

He peered through the wisp of his memory at the highway ahead. A handful of men struggled with a felled tree, to either stretch it across the road in ambush, or remove it from the road for easier passage. "Keep calm, *belladonnas*, remember you are with Cavimi Astimio. I promised I would see you to Bonne, and I shall. I will ask you to leave the conversation to me, and don't fret, no matter what words I may say." As he spoke, he spied the splintered trunk of the felled tree and recognized the short, bladed planes embedded in the wood, the tell-tale signs of an employed axe.

The men were setting up an ambush. Perhaps for travelers such as he and his charges, for to steal their coin? Yes, for coin. Like the Omen-Readers, hungry for more coin than they can spend and lusting for more than they can wench. *This will be a fun diversion from the drudgeries of traveling on foot.*

"Ho there!" Camimi called out, a cheerful wave to his arm. "Do you know the day?"

The thieves twittered like chickadees until one stepped forward. "The day? Why the day is Midestan! And my poor fellow, you have walked into a trap."

Cavimi laughed. "Midestan you say? Strange, I thought it Endweekstan. Ah well, that is most unfortunate for you, my dear Master Thief."

"Unfortunate for us?"

They were close enough now that Cavimi could see the whites of their eyes. He signaled for the girls to stop and pulled his blade from its sheath. "Yes, you see, I do not kill on Endweekstan, for I am a very religious man. But as you point out that this is

Midestan, I can kill without angering my gods. Who shall be first?"

"You think to take us all? Ten young men in our prime against an old man, a slack-jawed boy, and a dainty dame? Are you touched?"

"Yes, I am touched. I have my gods on my heel and in my hand, and I make you this promise. I can kill you before you draw your sword, Master Thief."

Cavimi saw the confidence ebb from the thief's stance and doubt take its stead. The thief shifted his weight and his fingers fidgeted with the grip of his blade while the others awaited orders or permissions. His struggle appeared endless, but Cavimi was patient. "Well, it is your luck this day, my friend," the thief said, "for we are waiting for a lordling's caravan. You are beneath our notice and may pass unhindered, so long as you leave your blade in your sheath."

Cavimi raised his empty hands for all to see. "Then we have an accord. May your score come swift and easy, Master Thief."

The girls followed him around the tree stump and beyond. Silence consumed them again until the sun dipped in the western sky. Belladonna demanded an explanation. "You're lucky they let us pass. We could have been killed!"

Do her eyes ever stop leaking? Cavimi shook his head. "Belladonna, did I not say there was no need to fret? Luck had no part in our escape. We were of no interest to the thieves. Do you want to know how I knew this?"

Artesia nodded along with her companion, her eyes kind for the first time since their journey.

Cavimi clapped his hands together with gleeful pride. "Well, first, there is the effort of felling that tree. I imagine it took the thieves a good part of the morning to do so. When one is setting up such an ambush, especially across a well-traveled road such as the King's Highway, one is trying to catch a very big fish. The kind of fish that will produce a large profit for everyone in one's gang of thieves."

He caught the ghost of a smile steal across Artesia's lips. "So, to spring such a trap upon an old man, a slack-jawed boy, and a dainty dame would have been foolish."

"Quite. I already let it be known I intended to fight. Whatever pittance they received from us would have to be won." Cavimi noted the sun's position and searched for a place to camp as they walked. "Now, in order to prepare for a caravan, they would need to dispose of our bodies and spilled blood so nothing would seem amiss, thereby warning the caravan."

"Ambushes only work when there is the element of surprise." Artesia said.

"Exactly. My dear, Artesia, you would make a fine soldier, so quick you are able to learn strategy."

They camped with a small fire that night. The meal Artesia prepared was hot and full of hearty flavors. And she sang prettily, as they bedded down, a foreign song of a soldier's plight and a bargain with a trickster god. And, while he slept, dreams of peace and wenching flooded his slumber.

"We shall be in Bonne this evening, if the weather permits and we have no more bandits to outwit." Cavimi announced on the highway the next morning. "And Belladonna shall be safe."

Artesia seemed content. "That is all the bargain required of you. When we reach Bonne, you shall collect your payment."

Cavimi whistled as they traveled. Pushing through the sunset hours, twilight found them road-weary and hungry. The guards at the gates of Bonne gave them little trouble and escorted them in. With the city gates secured behind them, Artesia turned to the weeping *belladonna*. "Hush, now. You are safe. Find your way to the castle and tell them who you are. You will dine tonight with the count and his courtiers."

"But your bargain! You have given yourself to this, this creature, and for me! However am I to repay that?"

Cavimi feigned a lanced pride. "My dear, Belladonna, you wound me so. And I thought ladies were above such insult. Is the castle where you are headed?"

Artesia nodded. "She is arranged to be wed, and her betrothed is a charge in the count's court."

"If you like, I shall escort you there, and you can rest assured that not only is she safe in Bonne, but delivered safe unto her betrothed as well."

Artesia smiled, but shook her head. "No, our bargain must be kept as it was agreed to. Belladonna can make the remainder of the journey on her own accord. And I hand myself over to you as payment."

"We agreed. I can do with you what I will?"

Again she didn't blush or flinch. "As is our bargain."

Cavimi licked his lips and offered his arm. "Then come with me, Artesia diPaccia. I know of a little inn near the harbor that has clean beds and a bath."

"A bath sounds delightful, if it is your will." Artesia accepted his arm and they parted ways from the weeping Belladonna, who had the sense to approach the gate guard for her escort.

Cavimi and Artesia strolled through the cobbled streets with heads held high, despite their tattered appearance. "Now that we are alone," Cavimi said, "I wish to know more of you. Why ever would a woman of your good sense and breeding subject herself to a bargain like ours?"

"It is my fate, my will, my destiny, my luck. It is what I am, whatever name you give it."

"That is not an answer and I do not believe in such things." Cavimi led her down another road, turning at a large fork headed for the harbor. "Why did you strike such a bargain with me?"

"Why did you accept such a bargain? When your rules are not for the nameless or the poor?"

"You captured my interest. At first, I was inclined to sell you at the slaves' market, for you, with your beauty, would fetch a high price. And now you will answer my question."

"I think first we will have our bath." Artesia said, pointing to the inn before them. "Then, if you still wish to know why someone like me made such a deal, I shall tell you all."

Cavimi made arrangements with the innkeeper for a room with two beds, for he still wasn't certain of his intended use for his payment. Artesia surprised him by catering to his bath. She massaged his forehead and his arms, sponged the grime from his back, and sang to him prettily while he soaked. Not once did she complain. Nor did she blush or flinch at the sight of his naked form.

Cavimi, who never once thought he would love or respect a woman, found he appreciated Artesia for more than her lovely form. The heat of the water infused his sore muscles, relieving stiffness, and the steam from bath made him heady. Perhaps it was the combination of the two sensations that made him feel so strongly for Artesia that he could no longer bear the weight of their bargain. "Artesia," he said, turning in his tub to look her in her eyes, "I free you."

"You...free me?" Her face blanched in the dim light, "What do you mean, you free me?"

He chewed his lower lip, puzzled. "I mean to say that you have fulfilled your end of the bargain. Your debt is paid. I release you from my, uh, command. You are free to leave as you will."

She swallowed. "You do not want this, Cavimi. You must rescind this."

"Why?"

"Because," her eyes glanced about the room. "Because of who I am."

"You are Artesia di Paccia, are you not?"

"No," she said. "Artesia di Paccia is the girl we left at the gate for her betrothed to collect."

"Ah, then you are her lady-in-waiting."

"No."

A metallic white light flashed between them and she cried out. Cavimi rose from his bathwater. "Artesia? Er, Belladonna, are you all right?"

"I cannot believe you would do such a thing." She inspected her hands as if they were free of shackles for the first time in her life.

"What hideous thing have I done now?"

"I am Jin. I was Jin. You…you set me free?"

"I did. But this Jin business, what are you speaking of?"

She slugged his shoulder. "You have never heard of the Jin? We were punished by the Omen-Readers for failing to meet our obligations to their order. They cursed us to spend an eternity in servitude to others for our penance. But you, you freed me?"

Cavimi shook water from his naked form. "I told you before. I do not believe in curses or in the lies of Omen-Readers."

"I have free will because of you."

He clutched her small hands in his. "Your free will is none of my doing."

"I wish to be yours still," she kissed his fingers, "I wish to do your bidding, for always and forever."

"I should tell you, I do not accept contracts with the nameless or the poor." He kissed her lips, hard and proper. "So what bargain shall you offer me in exchange?"

The Request

fiction by

Valerie Boersma

On this particular afternoon, a glimpse beyond the daisy scattered avocado and gold barkcloth curtains framing my front window might lead a casual observer to surmise that the woman who has come to visit me is an old and dear friend. That assumption would be partially correct.

In truth, the arrival of Mary Jane's letter a month ago, addressed to me in lacy blue cursive, was a complete surprise. Though we'd been college acquaintances more than two decades earlier, in the interim between the twenty somethings of our youth and where we found ourselves now—the forty somethings of approaching middle age, we had not kept in touch. The letter, penned on plain cream stationery, informed me of her plans to travel west and spend a month with her ailing mother and, furthermore, the route she'd mapped out would take her right by my town. Could she stop for a short visit? In all honesty, I felt more than a faint sense of dread, rooted no doubt in the nagging question: what on earth would we talk about? I hadn't seen Mary Jane for twenty-five years, and I doubted we had much in common. Despite my misgivings, I wrote back with a reluctant yes.

In the spring of 1943, there were 37 of us, including Mary Jane Brady, enrolled in the Fundamentals of Home Economics course. Even after all this time, I am able to recall the names of a few of my classmates. Lila May Martin. Alberta Parry. Muriel Maddock. Dorothy Scott. Marsha Wood. And if I've forgotten more names than readily come to mind, I can picture most of their faces. The one exception is Mary Jane. My recollection of her is as complete as the day we first met: dirty blond mop of wildly petulant curls; plain, almost matronly clothing; and soft spoken demeanor. So painfully shy was Mary Jane that she seemed perpetually poised on the edge of anxiety, and I sensed that making friends was not a skill that came easily for her. The art and science of baking seemed to vex her as well, and when it was obvious that her own bowl of flour, lard, salt and water was mixing up into a frustrating failure, I introduced myself and offered to share my own pie crust expertise. After that, she always seemed to want to cling to me, like ivy on a brick wall.

I'm perched tensely on the sofa, waiting for Mary Jane to arrive, wishing I had a few days left before her visit, and at the same time wishing this afternoon had already passed. I can't stop puzzling over her desire to see me, and I wonder how many other girls from college she's gotten in touch with. I hate to admit my own callousness, but I know that if I was in her place, I would not have written. It's not that I don't want to see her. I simply have no desire to relive my university days. Life has raced forward, and I, without regret, have tagged along with it. I suspect, however, that Mary Jane might be suffering from an attack of nostalgia, and by way of this reunion she is hoping to recapture part of her lost youth. A pang of empathy for Mary Jane stabs me. Growing older can be such a bitter pill.

Mary Jane's steel blue 1964 Olds pulls up in front of my house around three o'clock. I watch, from behind the cover of the daisy curtains, as she opens the driver's side door and climbs out. Her hair is very short now, those unruly curls professionally tamed, and she is wearing a piquant turquoise wool dress and coat ensemble, single strand of pearls, and black sling back heels. She looks nice. Very chic, in fact. Moving closer to the front door, I hover, waiting for her to ring the bell, but my nerves, coupled with a desire to get the ice breaking hellos over with, get the better of me. I hurry outside, meeting up with Mary Jane on my front walk. She sees me, calls out my name, and rushes towards me, wrapping her arms around me in the biggest hug I think I have ever had. I invite her to follow me inside, taking her coat as I show her into the living room, and I offer her coffee and dessert. She accepts, perhaps a little too eagerly. I sense she's as anxious about this reunion as I am.

A few short hours later, as Mary Jane's visit draws to a close, the unexpected has happened. Between bites of pineapple upside down cake and sips of Maxwell House, the two of us have slipped into easy conversation, chatting comfortably like best friends who have only been away from each other for days, not decades. I've discovered that I have a lot in common with Mary Jane after all and, more importantly, I find that I really like her.

As we walk out to Mary Jane's car, parting is genuinely bittersweet. I feel like I've found something precious, only to lose it again, and my grip on her shoulders is tight as I embrace her.

"Please, let's keep in touch!" I'm pleading with her, and she nods happily along with her reply.

"You can count on it. All these years, I've thought about you often, and how lucky I was to have you for a friend. You were so nice to me. Nicer than anyone else, *and* when I needed it the most. I've never forgotten that." Poised there, as Mary Jane lets go of me and slides behind the wheel, I suddenly understand why it was so important to her that she see me again. It wasn't about trying to recapture lost youth or wanting to turn back the hands of time. It wasn't about nostalgia. Years ago, when we were young, and the world seemed bent on defeating Mary Jane, I made her feel like she mattered. She's wanted to thank me ever since. It's a humbling revelation, and I am on the verge of tears.

Through misty eyes I watch Mary Jane drive off into the evening, both of us waving until her car is swallowed by distance and shadows, and I know that this ache in my heart will be with me for a long time. Despite the slight chill in the air, a sensation of warmth washes over me—the brand of warmth that comes from spending time with a very old and very dear friend. And although Mary Jane might think that she's the lucky one, she's got it all wrong.

I'm the one who's lucky.

On the Shelf
fiction by
Angie Kinghorn

Armed with freshly brewed tea, Matilda sat down at her desk with a sigh. All she wanted was sleep. But with only ten chapters of mediocrity, sleep would have to wait. She sipped her tea and turned back to Edmund and Katherine.

"Kat, I—"

"Don't call me that! I am not some scraggly feline you found in an alley!" Katherine, already dressed for dinner, flushed with anger. "I'm your wife! If you've got to call me something other than 'Katherine,' how about 'darling' or 'my love' or 'sweetheart?'"

Matilda groaned.

"God, that's utter crap."

Her phone trilled. She located it under a pile of clippings on 1910s fashion and hairstyles.

It was her agent.

"Hi Eileen," she said.

"Matilda! I just wanted to make sure we're on track for the 20th."

Eileen's voice was machine gun rapid, and Matilda's head began to ache. The 20th was less than a month away.

"Well, I was thinking of making some changes. Things are so...stale. I want to keep the series going, and to do that I've got to change something. Which means I'll need a bit more time."

"Well," Eileen paused. "I trust you. God knows I should by now. Matilda Livingston and the Percivals have quite the following, and I intend to keep it that way. So if you think it needs change, do it."

"But can we can push the deadline back?" Matilda pleaded.

Silence. Long enough that Matilda checked to see if her phone had dropped the call.

Eileen sighed. "I can give you a few more weeks. We've already postponed it once, and we need to get it on the shelves before the Christmas season. So write me something amazing, and do it fast."

Click.

Matilda stared at the phone. "Where's my Muse?"

A cold nose nudged her leg, and she laughed. "There's my sweet boy! Let's get out of here."

It was a crisp day in Manhattan, and Muse took the lead, sniffing the air. Matilda loved the freedom he gave her. Potential muggers would never look at him and guess that he slept in her bed every night and lay by her feet most days as she wrote. They just saw a "move on to the next target" sign, and that was fine by her. Muse was the perfect antidote to the hermit-like tendencies generated by her writing lifestyle, and the only reason she ever left her apartment. He had to be walked, which meant she had to get fresh air and didn't always eat leftover Kung Pao chicken.

"What should I do with them, Muse?" she asked. He cocked an ear, but didn't respond.

"The whole storyline is stagnant. Maybe Katherine should be pregnant? Or Edmund could have an affair with Ivy?"

Muse stopped to water a lamppost.

"You're right. That's awful. Oh, God, that would never happen. What about time travel? It's all the rage right now with period novels."

Muse stopped and squatted on that idea.

"All right. It's far-fetched. I'm just brainstorming here, okay? What do you want me to do? Have them leave England?"

Muse barked.

"Really?"

He barked again.

"Ok...well, I guess I could put them on a ship for America."

Muse put his nose in the air and trotted forward. On the way back to her apartment they stopped at the corner coffee shop. Mick, the proprietor, decided years ago to place Muse in the guide dog category, so he was always allowed in with Matilda.

"Mattie! How's it going? Hey, Muse!" Mick waved, his face red from the steam of the espresso machine. "You got that next one written yet?"

"Working on it," she said, digging in her wristlet for cash.

"Mattie, just put your rear in the chair and write. You're a pro." He began making her usual hazelnut latte with efficient movements.

He handed her the latte, and she was touched to see he'd made a heart with the foam.

"Look at you, getting all fancy!"

"Only for my favorite bettys," he said, handing her a chocolate croissant in a paper bag. "Now go kick some ass. My ma's book club will riot if you don't."

She settled at an outdoor table with Muse at her feet, occasionally lapping from the bowl of water Mick kept for him. What to do with the Percivals? They were on the cusp of happily ever after, and nobody wanted that, except for endings. This was not an ending.

"Yep," she said to Muse. "I'm putting them on a ship from England to New York. Edmund will get bored with Katherine and fall for one of the other female passengers." She chewed, pondering. "Who, though?" Muse gazed at her dolefully.

"He's ambitious. Let's put a princess on board and have him fawn all over her. It'll be *quite* the scandal." Energized, she grabbed the leash. "Let's go, buddy. We've got a lot of work to do."

She wrote through the night, bankrupting the Percivals and sending them out of England in disgrace. They headed to America for a fresh start, as Katherine had relatives there. She put the last of their money into first class tickets for the couple and their remaining servants: Katherine's lady's maid,

Ivy, and Edmund's manservant, William. She wrote Princess Sophie of Sweden into life, and, within minutes, Edmund was drooling over her royal petticoats (and coffers).

Katherine and Edmund were at odds and the story developed tension. Satisfied that it wasn't going to plunge off the bestseller list, she surrendered to exhaustion and went to bed.

The next morning Matilda took Muse for a walk and stopped by Mick's for breakfast. She was excited about getting to the keyboard. Muse could sense her enthusiasm; his ears pricked up and he wagged as they headed back to the apartment.

When she opened the door, she was assaulted by the overpowering smell of rosewater. She turned to see Muse frozen and growling.

Growling at an enormous pile of steamer trunks.

"What the hell?"

"That's exactly what I'd like to know!" A tall, slender man in a waistcoat appeared from her bedroom. "How dare you uproot us from England! America! As if we'd really want to go to the land of the nouveau riche."

"Edmund?" she said, faintly. "How...how are you here?"

"I'm here because you decided to take us away from Percival House and send us across the bloody Atlantic! Thanks to you we're homeless!"

Matilda ran to the bathroom. Where was it? She knew she had some left. Tearing through the drawers beneath the sink, she finally found the bottle of Valium and swallowed one. *Deep breaths*, she thought. *You're under a lot of stress. Deep breaths.*

"Really, was this necessary?" A cultured female voice came from right behind her. Matilda shrieked.

"Katherine?"

"Yes." She removed her large hat and gazed around the bathroom. "Where is your lady's maid? I *must* get out of these clothes. Ivy's seasick and managed to spill an entire vial of rosewater on me while she was dressing me this morning. Imbecile."

Matilda yanked open the door and ran out of the bathroom. Muse was still growling at the steamer trunks. With a snap of her fingers, he followed her into her bedroom, where she swallowed another pill before climbing into bed and pulling the covers over her head.

"I don't understand what you'd see in a strumpet like that, even if she is royalty!"

"Madam, it is not yours to question, but to obey. Kindly shut up."

"I will not shut up, Edmund! How dare you speak to me that way! I'm not some scullery maid; I'm your wife!"

"Then you should support me in all my endeavors."

"Even if those endeavors include seducing a princess for her money?"

Matilda cracked an eyelid and saw two figures sitting on the sofa. *No, it was a dream. It was a dream. Wake up. Wake up, Matilda.* Dammit, *wake up!*

"Perhaps we should ask Ms. Livingston to kindly return us to our previous living conditions, and none of this will be an issue."

"Right," Katherine agreed. "Ivy, wake up Ms. Livingston and then bring us tea in the...well, I suppose I'll have to call it the drawing room. I've never seen anything like it."

"Yes, m'lady."

The door opened and closed and the voices resumed arguing in her living room. Matilda risked opening her eyes again, and saw a young woman in a traditional housemaid's uniform, seated on the very edge of the sofa.

"Ivy?"

The girl looked up.

"Yes, m'lady. How are you feeling? You had an awful fright this morning."

"How...how are you all here?"

"What d' you mean?" Ivy's pale face was perplexed under her mobcap. "You wrote us out of England."

"Yes, but you're supposed to be on the *Lusitania*, not here!"

"That I can't say. I only know his lordship and her ladyship are most aggrieved at their current circumstances and want you to sort it out."

Matilda groaned.

"Let me fix you some tea."

"Absolutely not. I can get it myself."

Ivy looked pained. "I can't let you make your own tea. It wouldn'a be right."

"Ivy, I'm not worried about tea right now. I'm worried that I've gone crazy! And about what we're going to do with all the steamer trunk and all of you! There's not enough room! God, this is just my luck, to have gone mad on deadline."

"Don't worry, ma'am. William's moving the trunks to one of your spare bedrooms."

"One of my *what*?"

Two hours later, Matilda convinced William that the empty apartment next to hers was not, in fact, a spare bedroom, and that he had to move the trunks back to her living room posthaste.

"I don't understand," Katherine said. "Where do you live?"

Matilda looked at the knife block in the kitchen and wondered what the punishment was for murdering home-invading fictional characters.

"I live *here*."

"But there are only four rooms! Where do your guests stay? And your servants? Why would you closet yourself in one room of a grand manor?"

"Katherine, it isn't a grand manor. It's an apartment building. Different people live in each one of these spaces."

Katherine was aghast. "You mean to tell me we are in a tenement? This is unacceptable! Edmund! Tell her to write us back to Percival Manor right this instant!"

Edmund started and hid an issue of *Cosmo* behind his back. "Quite right, Katherine." He paused and looked around, as if noticing the size of the apartment for the first time. "Where will the servants stay? Where will we stay? For that matter, where are your servants?"

"I live alone, you insufferable idiots! And nobody has servants!" Matilda stalked into the kitchen and took a giant bag of carrots out of the crisper and scrubbed them under the faucet.

Katherine spoke first. "But you're not old enough to be on the shelf! And how do you dress without a maid? Not to mention your hair!"

"Whatever it is you need from the kitchen, surely I should be doing it," Ivy said.

Matilda flipped on the juicer, and the noise drowned out their jabbering. She poured a glass of juice.

"There's plenty extra. Make yourselves at home. I've got to write."

She sat back down at her desk, put on some Enya and sipped her juice.

Once the porters finished moving their steamer trunks and hat boxes into their first class quarters, Katherine collapsed on a settee with a sigh. "Darling? I'm exhausted from the trip over. I think I'll have a quick lie-down before dinner."

Edmund looked up from the papers he was scanning. "Fine. I'll tell Ivy to wake you when it's time to —"

"What the bloody hell *is* this?" Matilda turned from her laptop to see Edmund with carrot juice dribbling down his chin, presumably where he'd spit it out. She bit her lip.

"Is this what you people drink? Where do you keep your scotch, old girl?" Edmund dabbed furiously at his shirt with an oven mitt.

"I don't drink," Matilda said. "And I need to write. If you want any hope of survival, leave me alone so I can get your next book on the shelves."

She turned back to her laptop and raised the volume on Enya.

"What is that racket?" Katherine hovered directly over her right shoulder. "And where are the–I hate to use the word–'musicians' making it?"

"Katherine," Matilda said, slowly, softly. "I've asked you, politely, to leave me alone to work. You are uninvited guests in my house and I am in control of your fate."

"Be that as it may, that noise is simply –"

Matilda changed the music to Metallica. Katherine turned and ran, a look of horror on her perfect features.

Two hours later, she reflected that perhaps she'd made a tactical error. Edmund and Katherine had taken over her bedroom, while Ivy and William set up camp in the closet the realtor had insisted was another bedroom.

Matilda fell asleep at her desk, and before she knew it, she was waking at dawn to the screech of an opening window.

She propped herself on an elbow and looked up as Ivy lifted a huge oriental fishbowl to the sill and heaved the contents out onto the street. Someone outside screamed.

"Ivy!" she shrieked. "Tell me you didn't use my great aunt's oriental fishbowl as a chamber pot."

"Begging your pardon, only we didn'a see anything else appropriate. I didn'a want to wake you. Where are your chamber pots, then?"

Several hours later Matilda's voice was hoarse from explaining the intricacies of the modern toilet.

Edmund would have none of it, insisting that it was "witchcraft," and that "God intended nothing other than a whirling vortex in the sea to behave in such a manner, and I'll be damned if I'll dangle my privates over something like that!"

Matilda threw up her hands and marched to her bedroom to change the clothes she'd slept in.

Ivy was right behind her.

"Let me help you."

"Ivy, I don't need help getting dressed."

"Surely you do, ma'am. However can you lace your own corset?"

Matilda shucked her sweater and let her jeans drop to the floor. Ivy screamed and covered her eyes.

"Oh, come on, it's not that bad." Matilda said, grabbing a clean pair of underwear.

"Ivy, what is it?" Katherine rushed into the room. "Oh!" she said, looking at Matilda, clad in a lace thong and bra. Then she fainted.

"For heaven's sake," Matilda said. "Edmund! William! Come collect Katherine!" She changed into a clean thong and wiggled into a pair of skinny jeans.

"Madam! You did not tell me you were running a house of ill-repute!" Edmund said, shocked. "We cannot be associated with such."

William stared. Matilda put on a clean shirt and turned on Edmund.

"This house is only of ill-repute since Ivy emptied a chamber pot onto the sidewalk this morning. Other than that, my lifestyle conforms to societal norms quite spectacularly. As for associations," she said, jabbing a finger into Edmund's chest. "*You are* permanently associated with me. Without me, you wouldn't exist. Also? I'm sleeping in my room tonight. You two? Take the sofa."

"No, you wake her up!" Matilda woke from a deep sleep to Katherine's shrill voice, standing right beside her bed.

"And what would you have me do?" Edmund whispered. "I can't control this dastardly woman!"

"Convince her to set things to rights. Tell her we'll rebel."

"We cannot rebel! She controls our behavior!"

Matilda stretched and got up. "Take the bed. Suddenly I've got the most terrible insomnia."

Sarcasm was utterly wasted on the Percivals.

She left them in her bedroom, the sound of their raised voices carrying throughout the apartment. She knocked lightly on the door to the closet.

"Yes?" Ivy's voice was soft.

Matilda squeezed into the room, where Ivy and William sat on the daybed, knees to their chests. Ironically, she thought, this was probably about the same size as the servant's quarters they'd have been allotted on the ship.

"Listen," she whispered. "Do you want to go to America by yourselves?"

William started. "What d'you mean?"

"I mean, your luck's about to change. We're talking main character future for you two. If you want it."

William shifted. "How would we earn money?"

Matilda closed her eyes. "Remember your backstories," she said.

"Oh!" Ivy exclaimed. "I trained as a midwife with me mam before I went into service." She turned expectantly to William. "And you?"

"Well, me dad taught me to build things. I was quite a good carpenter, really."

Matilda nodded. "Exactly. You have everything you need to make a life for yourselves."

"But the Percivals..." Ivy said.

"I'll take care of that," Matilda said. "Good night."

Edmund and Katherine were still arguing, and her resolve strengthened. She opened her laptop. *This is the right thing to do,* she thought. *It will revive the series with more sympathetic characters. Besides, I can't spend another moment writing Edmund and Katherine. Or with them.*

Mind set, she opened her manuscript and changed the date of their voyage to April 10, 1912. Then she changed the name of the ship to *Titanic*.

Immediately, the noise from her bedroom ceased.

William pulled Ivy across the lilting deck toward a lifeboat.

"Come on!" He screamed, "We've got to go now!"

"*But what about Lord Edmund and Lady Katherine?*" *Ivy yelled.*

"*They're lost!*" *William tugged at her arm. "Ivy, come with me now, or, I swear, I won't survive. I love you.*"

Ivy threw herself into his arms, and he carried her onto the lifeboat.

Hours later, salvation came in the form of the Carpathia.

Matilda grinned and closed her laptop, finally confident that this installment would end up on the shelf.

Dancing Through Landmines

memoir by

Jessie Bishop Powell

"It is *not* my ballet day." Sam crossed his arms over his naked chest.

"Honey, you love ballet."

He did not say, "Screw you, Mom," but the glower he delivered certainly conveyed that emotion. It happened fast. One week, he worshipped Miss Kyana, and the next, he was at odds with dance. And he was adamant. "I don't like ballet. I can't do that. I hate ballet. I want to go home. I don't want it to be my ballet day." I suspected, though there was no way to be sure, that his disorders had stolen away his love.

It wasn't only ballet either. He stopped working puzzles and playing video games. He barely wanted us to read to him at bedtime, and his trains got minimal mileage. He could hardly even sit still to watch DVDs. It was November, and his emotions had been going down the toilet since late May. He was approaching a nasty kind of rock bottom. At age four. Giving up on puzzles and books bugged the hell out of me. But the ballet was the worst, because it put me in an absolute quandary.

I'm not the sort to force a kid to keep up with an activity whose time has passed. Sure, as the kids age, I'm going to make them finish commitments. But even a typically developing four-year-old changes interests as fast as he can flush the toilet. Sam struggles with a combination of Asperger syndrome and enough behavior disorders to write his own little psychiatric manual. I'd have been kidding myself to think those things, especially the behavior disorders, wouldn't play a role in his activities. There was no reason to keep him doing something he had ceased to enjoy.

Except I didn't think he had really ceased to enjoy it. I thought he had become so defiant that he even had to defy himself. He contradicted everyone about everything. There was one whole week that I derived bleak amusement from asking him, "Are you Sam?" just so I could hear him shout, "No! I'm *not* Sam. I'm Sam!" And he wasn't being funny at all.

So it was no real surprise that our attempts to get him to ballet on time and dressed were colossal disasters as soon as he decided he was done with the activity. Once he got in class, he was sort of okay, but, ultimately, we started keeping him out because we worried too much about what he might do.

But then, in direct contrast, at home, he would beg me to hunt up a particular YouTube video of Aaron Copeland's *Rodeo* featuring the Colorado Ballet. Or various combinations of "The Dance of the Sugarplum Fairy" and the Russian Dancers from *The Nutcracker*. He had options on obscure alt rock, well known classic rock, and everything in between. He could have picked The Stones, The Beatles, The Sweet, The Travelling Wilburys, or The Black Keys. But he chose to watch ballet. He would look while the dancers jumped and spun, and we would ask him, "Can you do that?"

Though his answer was sometimes a defiant, snarling, "No," it was far more often a yearning, "Not yet." And the hell of it was that the real answer was "Yes". He actually *could* perform powerful four-year-old versions of nearly everything those dancers put out there. He could do that wicked cool thing where the danseurs jump up straight legged and touch their toes. He could gallop sideways. And when he thought we weren't watching him, he was still doing those things in secret.

And then Miss Kyana called. "We're making a ballet calendar, and we need a little boy in a picture. Do you think Sam could come?"

Okay, let me be clear. They did *not* need a little boy for a picture. Or if they did, they had two other really cooperative little guys who could have served the role. They asked for Sam because they wanted to engage him when he was so desperately strung out. Did I just write that my four-year-old was strung out? Jesus.

The day he went, he could not have been less cooperative. He refused to do poses. He refused to dance. He refused to sit still. In the end, they somehow got exactly one picture of the back of his head as he watched a danseur leap. I really didn't think it would be a good photo. But it was. I certainly didn't expect them to put it in the calendar. But they did.

And after that, he was receptive to the words "ballet" and "day" spoken in the same sentence. So I took him back. First, I let him sit and watch for the whole session. "You can wear your school clothes." He didn't act out at all. Then, I made him get dressed, but still let him sit and watch. Finally, after a month, I told him he had to dance.

And he did. With only minor moaning. Part of the reason was that he had started mild medication, and he was *finally* improving. But part of it was that he had backed himself into a corner with all of the "I can't" and "I won't" garbage. After saying he hated it, he needed to be pushed to continue so he could save face. At Christmas, when we hung the calendar on his wall, he gazed at it, his face and arms wide open to the dance.

For the recital that year, Miss Kyana made him The Beast in his little class's rendition of *Beauty and the Beast*. I somehow never figured out beforehand that he would be dancing to Disney music. So when Angela Lansbury's famous song came on, all my air escaped, and my chest felt like someone was tightening a corset. I love *Beauty and The Beast*. It's one of the only princess movies that I enjoy without reservation, and the music has always captivated me. And that song? It hit me where I didn't expect it.

Then Sam skipped on. All by himself, he completed this elegant spiral, then gestured to the wings with professionalism I would have expected of a kid six years older. There was a moment when all three children did a graceful little step to the left in perfect synchronization, and the audience 'ahhh'd'. There was a truly talented little girl in the group, and, with only three kids in the class, Miss Kyana could really concentrate on each of them more. So there are clear reasons why his little trio was lightyears ahead of the others in the same age group. But it still took my breath away.

Miss Kyana *knew* what Sam had been through. She *knew* how apt the beast-to-prince characterization was for him. (Only, unlike the movie, he goes back and forth between the two personalities, even now.) She gave him that dance as a gift, a profound symbol of how far he had come.

But he still had ground to cover. Not two weeks later, just when he turned five, he jumped out of my moving car and bolted through a busy hospital intersection. The rock bottom I had seen coming all year rushed up to meet him with the holy wrath of inflexible asphalt. Physically, he was unharmed. Emotionally, he and I will both be scarred forever.

But good came of it. Until then, his medications had all been mild, with an eye to minimal intervention. Jumping out of the car qualified as a suicide attempt. The psychiatrist prescribed mood stabilizers.

The results were sudden and stunning.

For the first time in a year, we saw our son. The funny little guy under all that anger, the creative thinker hidden under all the frustration. He still had meltdowns (still *has* them), but they lasted a few minutes instead of a few hours, and he understood the gravity of his actions. For two weeks solid, he apologized every day for jumping out of the car. (Note: I accepted every one, but I didn't discourage the thinking-through that he was doing.) All summer long, he stabilized, and when school started back, a new school, this one a good fit, I could finally say my son was happy.

And then ballet came back around. We got an e-mail asking kids to come audition. There was one part for a kid age five to eight. I told Sam Miss Kyana wanted him to come dance. He was good with that. If I told him Miss Kyana was hoping he'd try out skydiving, I'd have to go pick him up at the airport.

When the children went into the studio, the new director came out and explained to the parents that he was really excited so many children had turned out. There was only going to be one part in this particular ballet, but he really hoped everyone would come back for *The Nutcracker* tryouts in September. He made it clear that he loved all of their kids and thought them all splendid dancers.

After the first round, seven kids got sent back out; all of them seven- and eight-years-old. The seven who remained were all six and under. Clearly, they wanted a younger child, since there's no question that the older students had more technical mastery than the younger ones. After another round, four more kids came back to their parents. That left three children. Finally, Sam and the last two little girls came out, and then Mr. Darren followed them. He said, "This was a difficult decision, because all three of you are really good dancers."

And then he picked Sam. The kid who had jumped out of my car four months previously got cast in a professional ballet. Because he didn't flinch in the part where another dancer has to put a hand over his face. Because he performed a lift without wiggling.

In the end, the part was modified to give two children a role, since Sam and another little girl had such good stage chemistry. They rehearsed for weeks leading up to the performance, and I made a point to stay out of the way. Sam acts better if I'm not on hand to show off for. Still, I wanted pictures, and I knew I'd be unsteady for taking them if I didn't do some heavy preparation. So I went to a rehearsal.

I walked in just as the dance started. Coldplay already permeated the studio. Chris Martin was singing a lullaby straight to my son. "Fix you" fit his life inescapably. Sam's part hadn't even started yet, but I was already dabbing my cheeks. After that, Adele got involved, and my emotions were completely lost. I should have brought a box of tissues.

The danseur playing the lieutenant general sat to one side in a chair. His ballerina wife threw herself forward in grief. And then the ballet corps rose up and pantomimed flying, flashlights aloft, bringing an imaginary man home.

For three minutes, Sam and Piper, playing the lieutenant general's children, waited on either side of the floor. And then they darted to center stage together in response to a cue I couldn't see. It wasn't the dress rehearsal yet, but the children and youth corps were costumed. Sam never looked my way. He watched the danseur, Vlad, the ballerina, Nichole, and his stage sister, Piper, as if they were already in the final performance.

As Sam ran in character, I superimposed the image of his red face dashing across the Baptist Hospital parking lot. By the time he jumped out of my moving car two days after his fifth birthday, we had been trying to fix Sam for most of his life. The little kid who arched out of my reach and lurched into traffic looked exactly the same as this dancing boy, but that child had a broken soul.

He had been to three preschools and one daycare. We took him out of the daycare before they had to expel him for biting. The first preschool collapsed under its own weight. Then we removed him from a second by mutual consent with the directress, because he was simply out of control. The third kept him on sufferance, possibly out of pity, or maybe because even at his worst, he had a charming smile. It was only this year, in Kindergarten, at a school for kids on the spectrum, that he was finding academic welcome.

Until then, only the ballet school never failed him. It boils down to this. For most of Sam's life, Scott and I have felt alone. We have dealt with educators who should have been reasonably expected to give Sam a chance who instead dragged him down. We worked with teachers who loved him very much who just couldn't help him anymore. We interacted with therapists, and counselors, psychologists and psychiatrists who had Sam's best interests at heart (well, and one who didn't). They were the ones who helped us get him turned around before his little train crashed. But, until Kindergarten, school failed Sam. Except ballet school.

Every class, no matter his attitude, Miss Kyana welcomed Sam. She nurtured his bright spark when others couldn't see through his clouds. Five months after his psychiatrist prescribed the first mood stabilizer, the healing showed everywhere, especially as he danced. We found a reserve of support where we least expected it. All year long, when there was no reason to think that they would or *could* extend flexibility to him, his teachers had Sam's back. In a world traditionally depicted as so conditioned and disciplined that art becomes more important than humanity, we fell into a deep well of loving kindness.

The music ended, and Mr. Darren said, "That was really good. I want to run through a couple of things with the little ones, and I'll see the rest of you tomorrow at the dress rehearsal. If you have questions, make sure you get them answered today before you go home."

The older girls departed, leaving a couple of the professional dancers and the youngest children. Mr. Darren turned to the little stage family. "Okay Mr. Sam, now you pull off a smart salute. Keep your wrist straight. Just like that." Sam stood at ramrod attention as Vlad lifted him high overhead and settled him on one shoulder, then picked up Nicole with his free arm. The ballet director smiled. "Good job!"

"Mr. Darren," said Sam. "I tried to practice at home, but Daddy can't pick me up like that."

Mr. Darren smothered laughter in his shirt. "Well, Sam," he said in his soft Australian accent, "Your Daddy doesn't spend his whole day hefting things."

Miss Kyana added, "These guys are picking us ballerinas up all day long. I feel sorry for them."

"I'll pick you up!" Sam immediately tried to hoist his favorite teacher by the legs.

"You're going to have to work out a little while before you can do that," said Vlad. "Lift weights all day like me."

I wiped my face on my sleeve. "Come on, bud. We need to get home."

"I want to stay in rehearsal all afternoon!" But he walked with me to the car. I felt the dancers watching him all the way out.

He yawned and stretched as I buckled him in. "Tired, bud? That was a lot of hard work you just did."

"Yeah."

I got in and started driving. He was quiet, so I thought he had nodded off, as he is prone to do in the moving vehicle. As we pulled into the driveway, though, he piped up from the back seat.

"Mom, I really love ballet. I have the best time with all my friends."

"I know, buddy. I know."

Fear

fiction by

Stephanie Ayers

Shallow breaths escaped the prison of my lungs as I stopped running. I stood at the edge of the forest, a dagger clasped tightly in my palm. The forest seemed cold, and I caught a hint of danger lying within it. The dirt beneath my toes sent shivers crawling up my legs, but I ignored them. A gust of wind burst from the forest and chilled me to the bone. I hugged my cloak closer to my body and sighed. Something was amiss. No birds fluttered from branch to branch. No songs breached the silence. Nothing moved, save the wind. My heart became a hammer beating against my chest. Droplets formed on my forehead despite the cool temperature. I knew my enemy hid between tree trunks before me, taunting me with its unseen presence.

I had to meet Fear—the only name I knew the beast by—head on. Fear, the unidentified foe that terrorized my village, lived within the forest. I was the only one who could defeat it. I had no kin to mourn me, no significant other to assist me. I was the next Luck to ascend the throne. I had to face this alone. My resolve evaporated quickly as I faced the tree line. My knees quaked, and I wanted to turn around. Foolhardy to take on this task, I knew I could not return until I had decimated Fear. Heralded a hero by the people, they would not welcome a coward back. I pressed my eyelids together, let my lips move in unison as a prayer fled from between them. I lifted my face and reached up toward Heaven, hoping the All-knowing One would reward me with courage. Filled with renewed strength, I took the first step toward the forest and the soil shifted under my weight.

A sharp odor, much like onions, filled my nostrils and refused to leave. *Fear*, my mind spoke. *Death*, my senses said. For all I knew, they were both right. No heady wood musk overpowered it. Moss had no scent. The deeper I moved into the forest, the stronger the smell became. Smoke billowed from the ground where smoldering leaves revealed the path I had taken. Finally, I saw footprints and realized it stank worst of all here. *Fear*, my mind echoed. A sinister giggle broke the silence and I froze.

"Show yourself, beast!" I shouted. My voice bounced from tree trunk to tree trunk deep into the forest until it was barely audible. A growl came from behind a tree. My dagger rose, poised and ready for attack.

"Show yourself!" I repeated, my voice as stern as a teenage girl's could be.

Light shifted in front of me. A flash of honey met my vision before it vanished. The ground vibrated as the beast ran. I dodged behind the nearest tree. Smoke spiraled up from places I had not stepped just ahead of me. Feet the same size as mine had just passed this way. Shuffling came from behind the tree where I hid and I held my breath. I counted to three then turned swiftly, swinging my dagger as I went. My hands found nothing but air. I still heard the shuffling, along with the giggling, though it sounded farther away. I stepped to the left, coming out from behind the tree, leaving myself open and vulnerable for attack. Nothing happened, however, and I quickened my pace. My eyes searched the ground for more footprints that were not my own. Successful, I followed them as quietly as I could, praying that my training as a hunter surpassed that of my prey.

The footprints led me to a clearing, one that looked familiar. I paused and took in my surroundings. Yes, I had passed this place already. The footprints were leading me back the way I came. Did Fear not wish to scrap with me, then? Ah! Could Fear be *afraid*? Another flash of honey filled my peripheral vision and I looked, only to find Fear had vanished again. This did not surprise me. I took off in the direction I thought Fear had gone and found fresh tracks, found freshly scorched leaves in the grass. These led me to a ravine and I rushed across, ignoring the bite of the sharp rocks on the tender undersides of my feet as I went.

When I reached the other side, the trail had disappeared. I climbed to the top of the ravine and looked down into the open space beyond. Barren and brown, it gave a sharp contrast to the bejeweled colors of the forest. No prints marred its surface, though, and I turned away, only to see the footprints moving south alongside the ravine. I berated myself and raced back across, following the path once more.

My ears learned the giggle of the beast, and I heard it before I saw it. I approached slowly on all fours, my intent to take it by surprise. The surprise was mine, however, when I came face to face with the beast, also on all fours. We were so close that had either of us moved one centimeter in any direction, we would have touched flesh to flesh. I scrambled backwards a foot, startled. It was a trick! How could the beast look just like me?

Fear wore its honey-colored mane in a single braid down its back, just as I did. Its wool cloak matched mine but for the muted colors. Its eyes blazed fire, unlike mine, and its gruesome smile gaped wide with sharp, pointed teeth. Were it not for the eyes and teeth, I would have believed it was a mirror trick. To make matters worse, it seemed to know what I would do before I did it, and we moved in unison. This made battle difficult. I could not win, and I could not return until I had.

Fear laughed, full and open-mouthed at my dilemma. Fear grew a foot, now towering over me. Fear raised its dagger of its own accord and moved to strike. I parried at just the right moment, and drew first blood, cutting Fear on the wrist. Pity that it was not mortal! To my horror, my own flesh tore. To wound the beast was to wound myself. The more I moved, the more I bled, and the weaker I became. I dropped my dagger as tears blurred my vision.

"Use your magic," a small voice said.

I looked up but saw no one.

"Observe your surroundings," said the small voice again. I moved my head slowly in a circular motion, making sure I caught everything within eyesight. Still I saw nothing or no one. Fear dived towards me again, and I inched backwards. Something stirred in the underbrush and caught my eye. Fear took advantage of my distracted state and lunged. A fresh wound gaped from my thigh, crippling me, and the weight of the pack on my back sent me to the ground.

My pack! "Use it!" The small voice said. I stared at the ivory rabbit hiding beneath the shrub. It hopped out of sight as if embarrassed.

"Silly girl, worrying over rabbits when you have magic to work with!" The small voice boomed louder this time, exasperation lurking behind its words. "Use the pack!"

How could I use my pack when my enemy was in front of me? To turn away could mean my defeat!

The small voice interrupted my thoughts. "You have the power to defeat Fear. Open your pack. Use the gift the wise woman gave you."

"I can't use that. It's my heritage," I said, only realizing I had spoken aloud when a butterfly took flight.

"Excuses. You were born a royal. You need no heritage. If you wish to defeat Fear and return to your people, that is the only way. The wise woman knew this day would come. She gifted you generously in preparation for it."

"I don't know how to use it," I said, my eyes focusing on the bush the rabbit hid under and from which the butterfly had taken flight.

"More excuses. Think! You have all the knowledge you need, child!" The bush shook slightly, though no wind blew.

My memories began racing as I stood. My recollection of my infancy was faint. I had not heard the story of the gifting in quite some time. My heart pulsated in a crescendo. Sweat slicked my forehead as the images formed. I closed my eyes, and my heart quickened. The rancid odor became stronger. Fear hovered close, yet did not touch me.

Carnation pink surrounded me. It hung over my head, shielding the light. It decorated the sides of my bed and up the walls that contained me. Peach faces studied me from above, their yellow and white smiles blending with the gap-toothed ones. A sea of sapphire, amber, and emerald orbs pierced through my flesh, scrutinizing all they took in. Gurgles and babbles flowed from their lips. One voice rose above the others, startling me with its shrill cackle. A woman, her black hair laced with grey, her face lined with wisdom, centered herself within my view. Adoration tumbled from her eyes and delight decorated her visage.

"This gift I give to you, wee child. Use it wisely, take great care' when wielded properly, it will triumph over your deepest fear." She opened her hand and revealed a small amaranthine globe. The crowd gasped as she placed the orb on my belly, but their fear was unfounded. The ball had no weight. A coo erupted from my throat as tendrils of warmth wrapped themselves around me. The wizened face beamed as her faced loomed closer and whispers tickled my ear.

"Your power will be great when the time has arrived. Know it, embrace it, and victory is yours." She reached in and gathered the ball. Her lips brushed its surface before they touched mine. Her breath reeked as she raised herself from my crib, the same stench I had become familiar with in the forest. It jerked my thoughts back to the present.

Fear lingered a mere breath away, an impish smirk on its face, its dagger ready to strike. Its arms stretched out and swiped at me. I stumbled backwards just in time. I countered aggressively, causing my pack to plummet from my shoulders. It landed on the ground with enough force to open and the ball rolled out. The flash of lavender against the green grass caught Fear's eye and it turned, hungrily, toward the sphere. Without thinking, I rushed behind Fear and sliced my dagger through the air. Amazed, I watched as Fear fell, its throat gushing crimson. Suddenly, the air cleared. The wind carried away the stench, leaving the sweet musk of nature behind. The sun broke through the treetops. My wounds healed. Only scars remained to remind me of my victory this day. It was at that moment that I understood the ball had done this. I did not know how' I only knew whatever enchantment was placed on it had set me completely free. Fear no longer had a hold on me.

Echoes of "well done" followed me as I walked with a renewed self-confidence out of the forest. I paused for a moment along the edge of the tree line and admired the peridot carpet and jade canopy overhead. The sun danced between the leaves, kissed the ground, and warmed my toes. Birds fluttered from branch to branch. Scarlet-breasted robins burst out in song, and the magpies soon joined them. A gentle breeze blew from the forest, shaking the leaves, and I smiled. All was right with my kingdom once more.

Positive Count

fiction by

Angela Amman

They hadn't bothered to release the curtains from their pulls before they'd tumbled onto the bed. Las Vegas hotels were designed to reach for the heavens, windows painted with bright lights that flooded rooms in a mockery of stained glass. Lips sought heat and limbs tangled together as they raced towards the release of tension that distracted Lola whenever James turned those honey- colored eyes her way.

For the first time, equilibrium remained off-kilter as they sank into the pyramid of pillows, and she fumbled for cigarettes in the nightstand. She'd been living in the hotel long enough that an overly generous tip would excuse the shadows of a single cigarette. Sulfur swirled between them as she wordlessly handed him the slim stick, eyes roving to the thin band of skin on his left hand, slightly paler than the rest of his golden hands.

He inhaled deeply, watching her gaze and pulling her close.

"A few days poolside should take care of that. Crazy how much lighter I feel without that little piece of metal on my hand." His relief was palpable, his words a promise.

Lola felt the weight removed from his hand pressed into her chest, and she held out her hand for the cigarette. She hadn't asked for promises.

His words continued, noise filling her ears. "I think she might have been relieved. Love is always something that meant more to me than it ever did to her."

She tried not to cringe in regret as he caressed her palm before passing over the cigarette. He was betting on someone he'd never understand, and she resisted the urge to smooth his hair back like a child's. Inhaling, she stained the white filter with red lipstick and lies, the glowing orange obscuring tears that threatened to fall.

"Baby. This isn't love."

"Maybe you just don't know what love is," he suggested, and her tears stopped as she heard the tone of his voice shift into hope. She didn't have time to quiet another man's belief that what he needed was almost within his grasp.

"Maybe." She stood, letting streaks of neon paint her naked body, his helpless gaze shifting any lost power back to her soft hands. A cardboard cup of coffee delivered a cooled shot of reality to what she'd promised herself she'd finish tonight. Somewhere in the desert, her father was making the same promises to a tumbler of scotch he thought was on the house, his bleary eyes trying to catch an edge of something that would show him how to finally collect the chips he'd been losing for decades.

Night pressed around her and she pressed back, caffeine awakening the parts of her brain his touch always dimmed. Seconds ticked as she slipped into the bathroom and smudged eyeliner and concealer around eyes that wouldn't close until after dawn. He slept, the feet between them growing by the minute, satiated by what he must have thought was an agreement from her.

Once, years before, when she still ricocheted into Vegas like a boomerang unable to stay away from the poison she'd yearned to escape, she'd contemplated colored contacts. Her own eyes were so pale they almost glowed in the blinking lights of the casino, and they seemed too much like a calling card. She defiantly rejected the idea, keeping them their own shocking shade

between sleet and the sea right before a storm; another snub, a challenge to a system with which she'd been playing chicken since she was thirteen. It was then that she'd realized she might be able to beat the odds the house always had on her worried, hungover, in-too-deep father.

Tonight she emphasized them, kohl and mascara contrasting with the ashen steel.

The familiar buzz of caffeine and adrenaline prodded her towards the door. Fingertips brushed over his skin, tracing pink patterns across his back before draping white cotton over him, sheltering him from the bit of Vegas she could control. Guilt and desire twisted together until she grabbed both key cards and tossed them together on the nightstand. A scribbled note followed before she could change her mind.

I told you this wasn't love.

Her angular letters screamed at her from the page, and she found herself blinking back tears as she forced herself not to soften the message with a closing. This sort of goodbye kiss called for a simple "Lola," but even bidding him farewell in his sleep left her unable to sign off with the name he whispered like a prayer. With time sweeping by on Saturday's accelerated clock, she agonized for long seconds before looping an "L" at the bottom of the page—a gift he might never understand.

Ice, Red Bull, and a little bottled water mixed into a tumbler, then a brusque click trapped James behind the hotel door she couldn't open any longer. Hundreds of dollars' worth of clothes and makeup and some not-quite-costume jewelry littered the room, a small price to pay for what she'd coax out of the casino tonight. The elevator ride was smooth, but she felt her arrival on the casino floor like electricity, smoke and desperation permeating the vaguely tropical scent wafting through some sort of manic air freshener.

Her fingers slid quarters into slot machines, eyes scanning and searching the blackjack tables. A complimentary gin and tonic warmed in her hand, her distaste for juniper ensuring her sips were small enough to nurse her drink until she abandoned it and ordered another. Feet stumbled, just a smidgen, as she wandered to a table she'd chosen twenty minutes prior.

She pretended to bite her nails at the table, though her teeth never quite marred the gleaming burgundy varnish. Bodies warmed the chairs on either side of her, the full table bouncing with the energy she needed to blend into the decadence of too many plastic dreams rolling across the green felt.

"I just love your earrings," Lola gushed, gesturing towards the oversized rocks dangling from industrial-inspired chains.

Two chunks of unpolished sapphire. Plus two.

Her eyes moved as quickly as the dealer's hands, and her brain moved more quickly than both.

She'd been nine when her father rambled for hours about card counts, about a month before her mother left for good. Minus one.

"Thank you! They were an anniversary gift," the woman explained, nodding towards her husband and signaling the dealer for another card. "Our eleventh, hence the steel chains. It's silly, but Stan and I always buy gifts from the list of anniversaries."

Eleven years. Plus one.

"That's so romantic," Lola's voice fawned as her eyes moved quickly, the number in her head shifting slightly up and down, her bets edging up as the number leaned on the positive side of zero.

"I like to think so. But really it's just an easy way for him to think of something to buy. I'm Joy," Joy said, pausing too long at her turn for her husband.

Beads of sweat trickled on the thoughtful husband's brow. Two, poised to drip towards his clenched jaw. Minus two. Lola's bet shrank.

"I'm Lola," she said, her small hand reaching from her purse to grip Joy's for just a moment, her head clicking up and down on a ladder with only a few steps, trying to keep her feet poised somewhere above even.

"I think we're heading over to craps. Stan's lost enough tonight at this table," Joy said, and Lola nodded in agreement, her laugh careful enough to avoid attention.

The drunk guys who took Joy's and Stan's places at the table were ridiculous flirts, and Lola shifted from friendly to vacuous, softening her eyes and lowering lashes.

"You staying here?" one asked, and she knew they'd said their names but only cared that the count had been positive since they sat down.

"Mmmm," she murmured, smiling and nodding towards the convention center. "I'm supposed to be here with my boss. He's got some meetings this weekend."

Two lies, of course, so minus two. Her boss was actually at a loss over how to deal with her particular combination of mathematical genius and utter boredom with her job. He'd been thrilled when she'd asked for a sabbatical before the ink dried on her Ph.D.

"Sweetheart," the blond one drawled. "You are way too gorgeous to be cooped up taking notes all day. We've got a cabana by the pool tomorrow if you want to come have a Bloody Mary in the morning."

Plus one semi-coherent pickup line.

"Tomorrow? You're not leaving already?" Lola teased as she slid more chips into her purse, careful not to shift the colored stack too low too quickly.

"Not if you're still playing," he said, exchanging a look with his friend.

"I'm always playing," Lola said, the words truer than the innuendo as she made a show of losing a few chips, again pretending to bite her nails.

Her wins were inconspicuous, her losses celebrated with an unnecessary sigh and furrowed brow. Perfect ovals nervously went to her mouth countless times but remained dark as blood as they tapped on the cool glass of gin and tonic, two limes each time. Every arc on every finger curved smoothly with each touch, with each gesture, with each measured tap, and though the people coming and going at the blackjack table never noticed, someone did.

The gold vest and skin tone tights slid into the background of expensively garish carpets and endless pinging dreams, and a waitress on the wrong side of thirty watched Lola unnoticed. Lola tipped generously but never met the waitress's eyes. She never met any of their eyes, not the wife prattling about her anniversaries, not the guy trying so desperately to hold her attention, and not the dealer trained to notice patterns of betting and winning.

Lola was losing. She proclaimed it with curses and sighs and more tinkling laughter and nails stealing into her mouth. Her chips dwindled. She sighed again, and the waitress was the only one who noticed some of those chips gently tipped, again, into the purse in Lola's lap.

Lola was winning. The unnoticed waitress knew it as surely as she knew Lola didn't touch the two limes mixing with ice at the bottom of each glass. Lola's eyes weren't meeting the waitress's or the dealer's or anyone else's, but they were trained on the cards flying around the table, and she was counting cards and the waitress didn't understand how the dealer couldn't see it.

And when Lola stood up from the stool, perfect ass molded into the seat, the waitress knew she had more chips in her little purse than the ones she'd sighed about losing.

The waitress paused, her tray leaning between her hand and the edge of the table. Every rule, every warning she'd ever heard about reporting suspicious behavior screamed in her head. Her mind raced, deciding between the pit boss and her manager, the bitch that poked at her waist tonight though she was thinner than half the younger girls here.

Lola swiveled, meeting the waitress's eyes with a smile for the first time, stopping when she saw what the waitress knew. Their eyes locked, and recognition that spanned miles and years combined with understanding about what Lola carried in her purse.

Then the waitress balanced her tray, squared her shoulders in her gold vest, and faded back into the carpet as Lola walked away from the table.

Lola counted steps, forcing her count past three as she moved forward, walking off the ladder of ones and twos and zeros that stuffed her purse with chips. Noise accosted her thoughts as she wondered how long it would take before a hand rested on her shoulder to speak with her about the rather suspicious chip collection she was toting in a purse instead of proudly carrying towards the cashier's office.

The hand never dropped.

Fists she hadn't realized she'd clenched unfurled, and she paused. Cash bought her a moment to think, in the guise of overpriced red wine and a packet of smokes she hadn't known she'd wanted until she felt her knees buckle in relief. Away from the table, her sharpened focus relaxed and her steely sparkle faded until she became anyone sitting at the bar and not someone with thousands of dollars in plastic sitting next to her Pinot.

Her next walk was calmer. Without the need to count her steps, Lola breathed deeply when she finally met the balmy night outside the artificial world of endless promises. The noise of the street couldn't muffle the click of her stilettos on the concrete as she strode around the mammoth body of the casino and sat on the ground near the employee entrance. She smoked steadily,

without thought to the havoc she was wreaking on her lungs but with immense regret over the damage the rough ground was wreaking on her silk dress.

The sun was almost up when Lola spotted the waitress she'd been waiting to see, and all four eyes were wary and weary and unsure why they were meeting at all.

"When did you know?" Lola's voice should have been hoarse from exhaustion and nicotine but wasn't.

"That you were counting cards? Or that it was you?"

Their words circled from lips to ears, almost whispers, carrying the weight of a past neither of them had really escaped.

"When?" Lola shouldn't have felt brave, but did.

"I've been watching people try to count cards for more than half my life. But I didn't know it was you 'til you turned around. Tommy always said he'd never forget your eyes. I guess I didn't either." Her voice was soft.

"I heard you and Tommy got married..." Lola started, but her words petered into the heat already shimmering around them.

"Yeah. He played at UNLV for a while, but I guess he never figured he'd have to do something besides play football."

"Are you still married?" Lola grasped for something that danced outside her consciousness, the kind of hunch her dad would follow for days and entire paychecks until he ended up eating two-dollar egg dinners with bloodshot eyes.

"What else would I do? What're you doing back here anyway? California has to be better than here. Isn't that where you went? Cal State or something?"

Lola bit back the correction. Why did it matter if it had been Stanford? Janine would still be standing here in a uniform that probably didn't earn her as much in a month as Lola made in a week.

Janine wordlessly accepted the cigarette Lola offered.

"Did you go to UNLV, too?" Lola chased, wondering why this conversation even mattered.

"Sure, for a while. When we got married I just kind of stopped. I always figured I'd have time, go back, you know? But I started working here, and Tommy started quitting every job he managed to find."

"And you never went back?"

"Not everyone gets out of here, Lola." Janine emphasized the name, and her words should have been bitter but just sounded like the end of an overnight shift that had lasted longer than Lola could have imagined when they were seventeen and sitting in a calculus class one of them never understood and the other one could have taught when she was thirteen.

Bluish smoke wafted between them, warm and stale and smelling like every memory she had of her father, every wish she made about turning her back on a city that twisted his modest ambition into something that paled under the false promises of fixed wagers. Not everyone got out of

Vegas, but maybe someone could. Lola opened her purse and pulled out the slim wallet, weighing its lightness in her hand against the chip-filled purse in the other.

Janine looked shocked at the weight placed in her lap.

"I imagine they have rules about you cashing in chips, but you'd be amazed at what a cheap wig can do."

"You don't need to do this. If I was going to report you, I'd have already done it." Janine said, grinding her cigarette into the ground with toes that had to be so tired of casino carpets.

"I know."

"Next time you might not get so lucky. Not every dealer's that blind."

Lola grimaced. "I don't believe in luck."

Janine smiled, shedding fifteen years with a genuine laugh. "Lots of people tell themselves that, hon, but you wouldn't be here if you didn't."

Lola stood, finally finished with something she'd started back when she'd first read her dad's battered copy of card counting guidelines. The crumpled pack of cigarettes lay abandoned as she walked in the opposite direction than she'd planned.

Her knock was hesitant and the seconds before the door opened felt longer than the entire hazy night. For an agonizing moment, he blocked the doorway with confused eyes, and Lola fought the urge to slide a teasing finger down his chest and apologize with sex and glittering lies.

"I thought you were gone." Lola could hear hurt and hope twisted together in his sleep-heavy voice.

"I lied," Lola said, the understated truth aching to unravel itself.

"Yeah?" He asked, pausing before reaching to slide his hand under her jaw. "About what?"

Exhausted, she leaned into his touch before admitting, "Everything."

"Let's start with the first one," he said.

Lola closed her eyes for an eternity, then met his gaze, wondering if there was any use in taking this chance.

"The first one? Well." She swallowed, wondering if there was any use in taking this chance. "My name is actually Lauren."

James stepped back, wrapping her into his chest.

"Nice to meet you Lauren," he whispered, and she followed him into the room to peel away the lies that had kept her from believing in a future built on his divorce and the desert sand.

Home Is A Table

memoir by

Nancy Campbell

We met our second family on a Saturday afternoon. Only in *Espana*, would I call my landlords my second family. But then, only in Spain does signing a lease involve *tarta*, *vino*, kisses and laughter.

We will be living in a small city, approximately fifteen minutes from my husband's work. It's a glorious separation, a place where the streets are narrow, the *fruita* stands are abundant, and the hours are Spanish without apology.

The owners of our rental home are about our age, with three children. Within moments of our arrival, my oldest and their youngest were in the backyard, in pick-up game of *futbol*.

"Is this a play date?" he asked, licking chocolate from his fingers during a frequent side trip to the kitchen.

Well, kind of. And kind of a business thing, too, I guess.

Yes, we signed papers and exchanged currency. But we also toasted with champagne. And red wine. Our new landlord made cake, spongey rings of lemon and miracle. The ladies of our rental agency brought olives and pan and cheese that should be illegal.

Our landlord and his family speak Spanish. We speak English. But we both speak parent, sound effects, and hand gestures. When my youngest drank a glass of sparkling juice, with much gusto, our landlord announced, "*Es Espanole!*" **He's one of us.**

Later in the conversation, I learned that *caliente* means "sexy" in Spain, and that if I order a *borracho* in a restaurant, I will get a drunk person, not a sandwich.

It felt good to laugh. We shared a table and a moment; we celebrated a beginning and a partnership.

The ladies of our rental agency, joy personified, gifted us with Spanish tiles spelling out our last name. For the rest of our lives, when we see it, we will know we are home.

And as we kissed our landlords and friends goodbye (one on each cheek, a tradition I'm slowly learning), I realized that home is a table, a smile, and *familia*.

Life doesn't have to be a checklist, and sometimes a Saturday afternoon is reason enough to welcome in joy and bask in the light.

Emerald

fiction by
AmyBeth Inverness

Emma hid her smug smile well. Mrs. Braisenburg was fuming again. The divorce proceedings were dragging out longer than anything Providence high society had seen since Jane Hutchinson tossed Stephen Hutchinson out on his ear back in 1901, sending him scurrying back to England.

"You know, you could sit down with Mrs. Braisenburg, explain to her that your relationship with her husband is purely professional..." drawled Ed, setting up the lights in the studio.

Emma grinned and dropped her dress to the floor, hoping for a reaction from Ed. No such luck. He looked at her naked form appraisingly, but all he said was, "That's not a sunburn, is it?"

Emma looked down at her breasts. "Nope. Just rouge." She started brushing the excess off. Perhaps she had gone a bit overboard with the make-up that morning. "And I feel no need to explain to that woman that I am a professional model, not a whore." Emma paused, then posed near the window, waiting for Ed to tell her to move away before someone saw her. He didn't. "And if I was sleeping with him, I wouldn't be a whore. I'd be a free woman exercising my right to be with whomever I please." She leaned out the window, somewhat disappointed that no one down below seemed to notice her. "Oh, look, the lawyers are here. Do you think they'll reach an agreement this time?"

Ed made a grunting sound and continued to adjust the lights. Emma sat on the windowsill and watched him. "You're doing it differently this time. Did he finish the last piece?"

"Early this morning. I don't think he's slept. He has something else in mind for today."

On cue, Mr. Braisenburg swept into the room, followed by a burly man Emma had never seen before. The man was pushing what looked like a lock box or safe. "Ah, my Emerald, my most precious jewel!" the painter exclaimed, embracing her with the same passionate kiss he gave any woman who would let him. "I have something wonderful in store for you today…"

The instant Braisenburg set eyes on his model, his Emerald, all thought of his fiendish soon-to-be-ex-wife were swept away. Emerald was truly a precious gem. Of all the models he'd ravished over the years, he'd never touched Emerald. Well, he'd touched her…he'd felt the weight of her breasts in his hands as he adjusted her pose; he'd run his hands appreciatively over her thighs as he admired her firm young flesh. But Emerald was different.

She was an artiste, both model and painter. She would be far greater than he was someday.

He spent hours changing the lighting and doing a few quick sketches before he decided on the pose he wanted to paint. Emerald glowed shamelessly, even though a half dozen assistants ricocheted around the room, following his orders. The naked girl may have seemed to be the most vulnerable of God's creatures, but she held more power than all the men combined.

"Mr. Braisenburg, they're ready for you now. And I'm afraid they won't wait," some lackey interrupted them.

Anger shot through him like lightning. Anger and frustration and helplessness. He would give anything—his fortune, his property, anything but his art—to be rid of his wife forever. She was intent on punishing him for his past and future crimes, affairs of both the body and the heart that he didn't regret.

Braisenburg stormed out of the studio. He only had one model at the moment, and all his wife's ire was focused on that one perfectly innocent young girl.

He hardly heard a word the lawyers said. He counted on his own representative to tell him when the offer might finally be something he could live with.

Then one shrill phrase from the harpy's mouth permeated his angry fog. "I'd agree to those terms here and now if only he'd throw that whore out on the street this minute with nothing but the clothes on her back." Braisenburg jerked his head towards her, scrutinizing her to see if she meant what she said. All the lawyers were glancing back and forth between the spouses, waiting for a response.

Braisenburg chose his words very carefully. "You will agree to these terms, if I throw Emerald out on the street this minute, with nothing but whatever she is wearing?" The harpy nodded. "And she will never return…" The harpy smiled evilly. Braisenburg leveled her with a glare, and she stopped smiling. "And you will refrain from calling her a whore."

"She calls me a flapper as if it was an insult," said Emma, making small talk with the painter's cadre of assistants while they waited. She couldn't even properly sit down, although they had artfully arranged for her to lean her hip on the arm of a sofa, one hand resting on an elegant bureau, and one foot scandalously propped up so her knees were wide. Her free arm was the one that bothered her. When Mr. Braisenburg returned she'd put it back into position, bent as if she was trying to scratch an itch on her back, but the arm was so burdened and heavy it was uncomfortable to do so for very long.

The conversation turned to politics, and how the better man had not won the presidential election. "Are you even old enough to vote, Em?" asked one of Ed's assistants.

"I turned nineteen on August 18, 1920, the same day the nineteenth amendment was passed," she answered. "Not quite old enough to vote yet."

"You will be the next time. You want to see Harding get another four years?"

"Hopefully by then I'll be in Milan, too far away to worry about American politics," she answered.

"Oh yeah, Milan; that's right… got enough saved up yet?" asked Ed.

"Not yet. Maybe by this time next year. I try to help out my folks too——"

They were interrupted by the sudden arrival of a dozen men in stuffy suits, preceded by Mrs. Braisenberg and followed by the mister. Mrs. Braisenberg stopped halfway into the studio, her jaw dropping nearly to the floor and her face puffing red with fury. She looked like she was trying to form words, but couldn't.

"Hello Mrs. B!" Emma chirped, waving her bedangled arm cheerfully.

The lawyers performed a comical pileup as they tripped over each other as soon as they entered the room and saw her. Emma kept herself from laughing, although a snort and a giggle escaped.

And Mr. Braisenburg, her dear darling Braisenburg, followed them in, almost skipping with obvious delight. That was strange considering the company he currently kept.

The starchiest, grayest of the lawyers cleared his throat. "Well…on behalf of the interested parties, and witnessed by…well, everyone…." his eyes stroked her body from nose to toes and back again. "Miss Emma Strickland is hereby banished from this house, taking nothing but what she is wearing at this very moment, never to return again." He took a deep breath, and blew it out, then took another. "And the division of goods in the divorce of Braisenberg versus Braisenberg is hereby settled, the finalization of said divorce to be December 1, 1920."

Emma stood up carefully, the jewelry weighing her down. "Really?" she asked, looking at the lawyer. He nodded. "Darling… really?" she asked, turning to the man who had already given her so much. The painter was leaning on the empty safe, dozens of velvet-lined drawers hanging open. She had no idea how much the jewelry she was wearing was worth, but it had to be in the millions. Every single piece in the safe, no matter how ancient or precious, was somehow draped on her body. Earrings hung from earrings. Necklaces piled on necklaces. She even had a few pieces tucked away in places that couldn't be seen, a private joke between model and artist.

One of the lawyers had laid his hands on Mrs. Braisenberg, restraining her just in case.

Emma shot her most impish smile at the older woman.

"You…" Mrs. Braisenberg began to yell, but fainted instead. Or rather, she delicately fell back into the handsome young lawyer's arms, one hand dramatically pressed to her forehead.

"Well then. *Ciao bella!*" Emma blew a kiss to the soon-to-be-former-Mrs. Braisenberg then danced over to her darling, the jewelry clattering and jangling all the way.

"My beautiful Emerald, how I will miss you!" he spoke with all sincerity.

She wrapped her arms around his neck and gave him a huge sloppy kiss. "Oh, darling, thank you so much. Not just for this…" she looked down at herself, then looked back into his eyes. "But for… everything."

She kissed him again, more slowly, then unwound herself and skipped off down the hallway. At the bottom of the stairs, she heard Ed chasing after her shouting, "Wait!" and waving a painter's tarp. "Geez, ya wanna get arrested? Or mugged?" he asked, throwing it around her shoulders.

Emma reached up and smooched him before he could dodge. "Thank you Ed. You're a heck of a guy."

Wearing the sheet like a cape, she danced off down the street, visions of Italy dancing in her head.

TAILS

Lucy

fiction by

Mandy Dawson

"I'm so glad you're here!" A small woman rose to her feet as Joan walked through the door.

"Of course I'm here, Maggie." Joan began to unwind the scarf from her neck. "Did you see it out there? It's freezing." She stomped her feet to regain feeling to her numb toes. "Why isn't she coming out?"

Joan crossed to the roaring fire and held her hands out to the warmth.

"She's been like this for days, Miss Joan." Maggie rushed to move a stool. "Sit for a moment. There's time."

"Not according to Father," Joan replied. She sighed in memory. Father had been in rare form this morning. Joan sighed. "I'll go up and see her." Maggie joined her as she left the room.

Joan looked at the woman walking beside her up the curved stairs. Her kind hazelnut eyes were set deep in a face crinkled with age and years spent outdoors. The smell of grass and fresh air wafted around her in an earthy perfume. "Has she been singing?"

Maggie shook her head, her face worried. "The sun hasn't been here in two weeks."

Joan patted the woman's arm as they came to a stop at a heavy oak door. "I'm sure it will come back."

Maggie nodded. "It always has before." She glanced at the door and lowered her voice. "I've never seen her like this. I think," she paused as if unsure how to continue.

"Speak freely, Maggie," Joan urged.

"She's starting to make connections. I think she realizes she's never going to leave."

Joan pushed down a pang of guilt. "Have you told her that?" she asked sharply.

"No, Miss." Maggie's cheeks reddened.

Joan felt the beginnings of a headache twinge between her temples at the lie. It appeared Maggie would need to be replaced. She'd inform Father. "I'll see what I can do. That will be all." It would have to be timed carefully. Lucy was fond of Maggie.

"If you need anything, Miss, just ring." Maggie left silently.

Joan took a deep breath and calmed herself before pushing open the door. It swung on silent hinges to reveal a girl sitting motionless in front of a barred window. The black iron circled in whimsical pattern but couldn't be mistaken for what it was. Clothed in a soft white cotton nightgown, the girl's back was ramrod straight in the wooden chair.

"Lucy?" Joan's voice came out in a soft whisper. She had hoped for a response. Getting none, she crossed the floor. Her shoes whispered on the thick rug. The intricate weave evoked brilliant blue flowers trimmed in shades of green and yellow. Lucy had fallen in love with it the moment their father had it delivered to the room. She'd danced across "her meadow" with a giggle of delight.

Joan looked around the room noting the changes two weeks had brought about.

The room was meticulous. A bouquet of lavender sat in a vase on the nightstand next to the bed, their calming scent a temptation to crawl between the crisp linen and under the thick down comforter that looked as if it hadn't been touched in days. Two weeks ago, that same bed had been a colorful nest of pillows and bright quilts with a laughing Lucy in the middle. Now the pillows sat neatly against the plush headboard in silence while the quilts were folded neatly at the foot of the bed.

Joan looked across the round room to the bank of large windows, bearing their own patterns of iron. A blank canvas sat on an easel; its emptiness was a contrast to the finished paintings leaning against the walls along the floor. Brushes sat neatly in gleaming jars lining a nearby shelf. A harp sat forlornly to the side with an air of neglect, the gold clear of dust but somehow dulled in the dreary light filtering through the curtainless windows.

The tidy room didn't reflect the usual vibrancy that was Lucy. Gone was the disarray that walked hand in hand with the tiny sprite who ruled the tower room.

Joan walked closer to the girl in front of the window. "Can you hear me?" She reached out a hand to touch the mass of raven hair that twisted down Lucy's back. Her fingers caught on a knot. Gently, she pulled the pieces apart, working the tangle free. "Lucy?"

Lucy gazed unblinkingly out the window, her eyes matching the storm clouds gathering on the horizon. Joan pulled her bag into her lap. "I brought you something, Lulu." She pulled out a tiny porcelain cat. "I thought it looked like Lewis." She placed it on the windowsill between a perfect miniature bluebird and a horse caught in the act of galloping. The cat's merry green eyes seemed to glance impishly at Lucy. There was no movement from the still figure. For a moment, Joan had the thought that perhaps Lucy herself had turned to porcelain. She shook off the uneasy feeling.

Joan reached into her bag again for a brush. She scooted closer to Lucy and separated a section of hair. Talking softly, she began to work the tangles. "Mother sends her best," she started. "She'll be by in a day or two..." Joan trailed off. "Lucy? Can you hear me at all?"

Joan picked up Lucy's pale hand, the fine blue veins making a road map punctuated by dark blotches. She ran her fingers over the half-moon nails, noting their smoothness. "Looks like you've gotten a manicure," she said absently. She stared intently into the colorless face of her sister. "Lulu?"

Joan closed her eyes and swallowed hard. She sighed and picked up the brush again. She continued brushing Lucy's hair in silence until it gleamed ebony in the dim light of the room. Outside the windows, the sky darkened.

"Much better," Joan sighed letting her hand slide through the silky tresses.

"Depends on how you define better." Lucy turned suddenly, catching Joan in the storm of her eyes. After so much time spent in stillness, the movement startled her. She put a hand to her heart to slow its pounding.

Joan had never been frightened of her sister. From the moment she'd been born, she'd been pampered and placated, each need met before she could utter a cry. There was nothing to fear from this child who was almost a woman. "What's wrong, Lulu?" she asked softly.

"You ask me what's wrong?" The words were hissed out of a perfect rosebud mouth. Rain began to beat against the windows. "That is what's wrong!" She flung her hand towards the windows.

"Rain is good for the crops, though we've been getting quite a bit of it lately," Joan said carefully.

"I'm not talking about the rain!" Lucy laughed bitterly. "I know where the rain comes from. How long did you think it would take for me to notice?"

"The bars are there for your protection. They've always been on the windows. There are those who would use you," Joan began.

"Because I'm special?" Joan had never seen Lucy sneer. The ugly expression twisted Lucy's face into a tortured version of her baby sister.

"You're very special and you must be protected," Joan recited as she placed her hand gently on Lucy's shoulder. She shrugged it off roughly.

Lucy tilted her head to the side and stared at Joan. "Protected or imprisoned?" she asked in an oddly calm voice.

"No, Lulu! Never imprisoned!" Joan rushed over the lie the family told themselves. "We've told you! You're our treasure."

"Then let me leave this," Lucy said reasonably.

"I can't." Joan forced her voice to steady. "This is truly the safest place for you."

Lucy stared at her. Hail began to beat the roof and windows. "Why is it safe for you out there?"

Joan felt the blood drain from her face. She linked her cold fingers loosely in her lap. "You're special," she said simply.

"Am I?" Lucy stood, her slim body rounded with the new curves of womanhood. "And you're not?"

Joan met Lucy's knowing eyes steadily. "I'm not as special as you are. I don't have your...gift."

"I'm your friend. I'm your sister." Joan's heart ached at the hurt and anger in Lucy's eyes.

"You'll have love and friendship and everything else you need. Father will see to it."

Lucy began to pace. The hailstorm intensified, the balls of ice growing larger until it sounded as if the wall and windows were being stoned.

"Father," she muttered. "You think I don't see what he does? You think I haven't realized? Father gives and Father takes according to his needs. And you," she spun on her heel and pierced Joan with a gray look, "you are the in between."

Maggie had been right. Lucy was putting the pieces together.

Lucy walked to the pile of canvases and picked one up. Gently she ran her fingers over the emerald paint. "I want to climb a tree. I want to ride a horse across the meadow. I want to swim in the lake I know is there but can't see."

"Well, to be honest," Joan forced her voice to remain calm, to distract, "Mother would have fits if she caught either one of her daughters in a tree."

"Have you climbed one?"

Joan hesitated.

"And am I so special that I'm to never know love or friendship?" Lucy's voice was filled with pain.

"Of course you have. Why wouldn't you? You're not as *special*." Lucy threw the canvas to the floor. She spun and resumed her frantic pacing, her hair flying behind her while the hailstorm picked up speed until the chunks of ice rattled against the windows without pause.

"Lulu, please, calm down." Joan stood and put her hands out to her sister. "It'll be fine. I'll tell Father to come see you."

Lucy turned in a whirl of white cotton and black hair. "I'm very calm," she said, the darkness of her eyes belying her words. "And I don't want to see Father." She stalked across the room towards Joan. Her eyes slid down to the pendant resting in the dip of Joan's collarbone. Joan resisted the urge to cover it with her hand. Lucy reached out with one finger and caressed the sky blue stone encased in filigree and suspended by a sturdy chain.

"It's pretty." Lucy lifted the pendant from Joan's skin.

"I like it. It was a gift," she swallowed and steadied her voice. She forced herself to stay still. "I was told it matches my eyes," she added lightly, hoping to bring her sister from the dark place she currently resided.

Lucy tilted her head in curiosity. "It does. It matches mine too."

"Not at the moment," she said evenly.

Lucy smiled in mimicry of her former sunny disposition. "It could." She twirled her hair in time with the wind whipping around the tower room. "We could trade places."

Joan swallowed. She hadn't expected this. No one had. "No, Lulu, we can't."

"Why not?" Lucy pouted.

"Because we can't. That's not how it works."

"Says who?"

Joan sighed and shrugged. "I don't know. Whoever makes the rules. Fate? Luck? Chance?"

"Aren't they all the same?" Lucy walked to the bed and sat on the edge. The wind outside the window began to calm. Joan let out a tiny sigh of relief.

"They're not. I don't know who decides these things." She walked to a small stool near the bed but far enough to have time to move if Lucy became unstable. "Just realize, you're here for your own safety."

"My safety," Lucy mocked.

Joan studied her sister and made a decision. She hoped Mother would forgive her. She swallowed. "I was stolen."

"What?" Lucy's eyes widened in shock.

"When I was very young, long before you were born, I was stolen. It took Father months to find me."

"How?"

"He is very clever. He just followed the storm clouds." Joan smiled a little. "We're fairly easy to find, you know."

"No. How were you stolen?" Lucy's eyes were wide with fear.

"I was playing with my doll in a meadow. Father and Mother were a short distance away. We were having a picnic." Joan smiled in memory. "Mother had made lemon cake. It's my favorite, you know."

"Mine too."

"They were laughing. Their laughter sent sunshine through me until I thought I'd burst from happiness."

"Where were the guards?"

"They were all around. I think, looking at it now, we thought the guards were window dressing, a precaution."

"Was it an army?"

"No," Joan shook her head with a laugh. "It was a little girl. She skipped between the guards and began to play with me. We sat in the tall grass and made daisy crowns." She smiled sadly at Lucy. "I'd never had a friend. When she began to walk away, I followed her. We held hands until we got to the edge of the trees. The men," Joan's smile faded, "were waiting for us. They gave the girl a candy stick. She smiled and waved at me, skipping away through the woods." Joan rubbed her stomach, which ached in memory. She could still feel the rough hands, still taste the fear as she watched her friend disappear. "I don't like thinking about it," she said quietly. "It's why they are so careful with you. You are so much more than I ever was. It's as if..." Joan turned to stare out the window at the rain falling more gently, "it's almost as if whatever was mine was sucked out of my body the instant you were born. You are that special."

Joan felt Lucy's hand on her arm. She smiled wryly at the change of places. "I'm sorry," Lucy whispered. Joan turned to hold her sister's hands.

"Don't ever be sorry," she said fiercely. "Not for taking it from me. I couldn't do it again. I'm not strong enough," she confessed. "But you are."

Lucy's eyes had begun to lighten to a pale blue. Tears slid slowly down her cheeks. "I'm afraid, Jojo. I'm afraid I'll never leave this place."

"I know," Joan wrapped her arms around her sister in a tight hug. "I wish I could say you will." She pulled away. "It will all work out," Joan said soothingly. "You'll see. In a few years, Father will start looking for a husband for you. He'll protect you when we can't. You'll have a happy life full of love and babies. You'll see," Joan repeated.

"Do you really think so?" Lucy wiped her tears with the back of her hand.

"I do. Father's already mentioned it in passing. We'll need someone to take care of you, you know. You're a handful," Joan teased.

Lucy smiled and ducked her head. "Can you be sure to tell Father to make sure he's handsome?"

Joan put her hands on either side of her sister's face, staring into eyes the color of the ocean after a rain. "Lulu," she said gently, "don't you know your happiness is the most important thing to us all? If you want a handsome man, we'll get you a handsome man. If you want a man with wavy blond hair and a dimple in his chin, then that's the man you shall have. Father will move heaven and earth to make sure you're happy."

Lucy's eyes began to darken with tears. "Does he do it because..." she gestured towards the window where a gentle rain fell. "Or does he truly want me happy?"

"Oh sweet! Of course he wants you happy!" Joan pushed down the guilt she felt in her part of the manipulations. Their father did want his youngest daughter happy, unless he needed her sad.

Lucy's mouth turned up in a watery smile. "Do you really think he'll get me a handsome man? Someone gentle and funny?"

"I think he'll get you the most handsome, gentle, funniest man he can find."

A small beam of sunlight slashed through the clouds and illuminated the porcelain cat.

"And I'll have babies?"

"Of course you will, silly girl. Fat babies who will make you long for silence." The clouds parted and warmth filled the room.

Lucy's eyes clouded over. "Do you think my babies will be special?"

Joan shrugged. "That's not up to us."

Lucy looked out the window. "Fate? Luck? Chance?"

Joan joined her, looking over emerald grass glistening in the sun. Sky the color of her pendant peeked between clouds lightened to the palest of white. She stood in silence, watching as the world opened to the sun. "You do that, you know. Without you, no one could survive."

"I know," Lucy said quietly. "I've always known."

Ricochet

fiction by

Megan Jauregui Eccles

When she finished washing the blood from the sheets, she started on the mattress. It frothed pink around her fingers as she tried to unstain what was once hers, as she tried to undo what had been done. He lay on the floor, his face a wound. She put him on her softest nightgown, the blue he loved so much. She would call the police as soon as it was clean.

They would tell her the ricochet bullet was a fluke, a 'never happens.' The news vans would eventually leave, carrying stories of disbelief and calculated punchlines to feed the masses about the man who died in a gun fight in his sleep. They wouldn't tell of her hands, cracked from bleach, as she tried to wash away what was outside and should be in. They would never mention the smell of his hair or the sounds of his voice or the touch of his calloused hand in the morning; all the things she couldn't live without, though she would try.

The parents of the boy who shot her husband came to the funeral. They stood in the back, but she saw them, recognized their guilt. They were in brown and gray instead of black, and she tried not to hate them for it. As she put her husband in the ground she recalled his laugh and how it caught in his throat. She recalled the way he used to kiss her, eager for the taste of her lips when he walked through the door. She recalled the words he said before his final breath. "I love you, my sweet. I'll only sleep so I can dream of you."

She considered flinging herself into the open grave, to sleep beside him once more. The mourners wept their way away with awkward high heeled steps and whispers of 'good man' and 'tragedy.' She wrapped up her tears and went home. It was an empty place, though it used to be full. Every corner of it contained a memory: the threshold he carried her over after their wedding day, the nick in the wall where she threw a plate at him during a fight over nothing, the room they would paint the softest shade of green, for a baby who would never come, the stain, now the color of rust instead of red, where he died.

She would never get it clean.

Rock and Glass

memoir by

Melissa M. Kirtley

Her screams woke me on a Saturday morning.

I didn't jerk back the covers or bolt out of bed. I didn't race to her room and throw open the door. I just somehow materialized in her doorway.

She crouched on the bedroom floor with her head between her knees. Her fingers gripped and yanked her hair, and her body trembled violently. My chest tightened against her anguished screams as she begged for God to kill her.

"Kill me! Kill me! Let me die! I hate this!"

In the distance, I heard another set of screams. A few feet away, my three-year-old brother, Aaron, cowered in the corner of his small toddler bed in terror. I stepped around my mother's fetal body, scooped Aaron into my arms, and took him outside into the chilly autumn air.

On the back porch, I wrapped Aaron in his blanket and whispered in his ear, hoping that my loving words would drown out our mother's scary ones. His screams subsided, but his fear did not. His lip quivered and his breath shook as he inhaled. My whispers grew louder as our mother's breakdown escalated inside. A neighbor's window slammed shut, and I wished I had a window to close.

I had offered my mother no comfort—not a kind word, not a touch on the shoulder. I did not ask her what was wrong or plead for her to talk to me. I refused to give her the attention she craved. This was a new manifestation of her illness, although I didn't know it was an illness then. To me, that's just how mom *was*. That was our normal.

Her moods had always swung from extreme happiness, to deep despair, to intense anger without notice. Mom could be laughing one minute and then throwing pots and pans across the kitchen the next, simply because she couldn't find the lid she wanted.

"Nothing ever gets put back where it belongs! I can never find anything in this house!"

Dad had moved out and Aaron was too young to put the dishes away, so I could only assume that her rage was directed toward me. One could never know when she would lose her temper or what would trigger it. Our floors were littered with eggshells.

"Mommy's sad again," Aaron whispered into my chest. "She scared me." His small frame curled up tighter against me as I rocked him back and forth.

No one was happier than mom when dad left. She had gleefully held the door open for him. I was sad to see him go, but after ten years of hearing them sling hateful words and slam doors, I figured divorce was the best solution for everyone.

Dad had been a stickler for a spotless house. Never one to clean it himself, of course, he made particular demands of how mom and I should do it while he busied himself around the yard, puttered in the garage, or played golf. After I dusted, he would run his fingers along the furniture to inspect my work. Sometimes I missed the narrow space on the shelf next to the television. He would motion me over, bend down to my eye level and say, "You see that, Melissa? How could you miss that?"

After dad moved out, mom's newfound independence included freedom from housework. She stopped worrying about how the house looked and seemed to draw great satisfaction from the sink full of dishes and overflowing hamper. "It's so nice not to have to spend our Saturdays cleaning anymore, isn't it?" she would say to me with a mischievous smile. I would smile back at my teammate and co-conspirator, just happy to see her happy.

A few months later, loneliness set in and mom began missing him. Her cries started out softly, muffled into pillows behind her bedroom door, and my heart ached for her. My fourteen-year-old brain couldn't make sense out of it. She had finally gotten rid of him, so why so much sadness? Wasn't this what she wanted? The family tried to support her any way they could, but they asked the same questions in confused whispers.

As mom's depression deepened, the house began to fall apart along with her mental state.

What started as a healthier, more moderate approach to housekeeping, had evolved into a concerning neglect. Gnats swarmed the dirty dishes, mildew overtook the bathroom, and cobwebs grew beyond just the corners. The giant mold spot on my bedroom ceiling crawled slowly with its long, black fingers, and I began to see faces and shapes in it, the way most kids stare up at clouds on a sunny day.

The bugs and vermin were the worst part. Large colonies of ants made their homes in the rotting wood and bravely strolled across our carpet like they owned the place (which I guess they sort of did). Mice darted out from behind the couch and scurried to the next hiding place, although some of them boldly ate crumbs right in the middle of the floor as if daring us to do something about it. They burrowed in the wall next to my bed, just a few inches of sheetrock separating them from my head. I had dreams—some sleeping, some awake—of mice eating their way through the wall and crawling on me. They rummaged through the small trashcan in the corner of my room at night and made a *thoomp* as they squeezed under my bedroom door.

I had always felt anxious when my friends came over because I never knew when my parents would start a war. When dad left, I thought, "Well, at least I can invite people over now." That bright light promptly fizzled as my home deteriorated and became a source of even greater embarrassment. I tried to keep up with the housework as much as I could, taking on the laundry, scrubbing our repulsive toilet and doing other chores without being asked. As the condition of the house worsened, so did mom's despair. It became a vicious circle with which I could not keep up.

At the family's encouragement, mom sought counseling, and that seemed to help for a while. Her mood lifted a little and she got some of her energy back. She spoke optimistically and openly to me about her sessions, and at first I thought of Therapist Greg as the savior our family needed. But soon, talking about her pain became an addiction. As if a dam broke, I couldn't stop her flood of words from coming at me.

My sympathy and concern slowly morphed into anger and annoyance. I grew tired of managing my mother's emotions, of walking a fine line, of watching my words, of holding my breath. I grew tired of being Therapist Greg's stand-in between appointments, staying up with her until the wee hours of the morning as she spilled her grief and tears into my lap. I quickly learned my role in these situations. I could not speak, only listen. I could not express any sadness of my own or even the cliché "I know how you feel." My words often got me into trouble.

"How can you possibly know how I feel?" she snarled one night after I made the mistake of telling her that I, too, missed Dad. "He didn't leave *you*, Melissa. You're the lucky one. You didn't lose your dad. *I* lost *my* husband!" My grief belonged to her.

Mom's pain replaced all the air in the house, making my breath shallow and hesitant. No one else was allowed to feel anything. Only *she* knew real agony or had the right to be angry. The world only had one victim.

Starting high school is hard. It's harder when your mom is going crazy and your house is overrun with mice and mold. Every morning before school, I meticulously chose my outfit, curled my hair, and put on a cloak of false confidence. I was pretty and popular enough, so people liked me. I got straight A's and stayed out of trouble, so the teachers loved me. I made the varsity cheerleading squad, so I got some attention from boys. I did my best to portray perfection so no one would ever guess what my home life was really like, and my disguise worked most of the time.

It didn't take long for mom to notice the differences between my life and hers. To her, I had it all—everything she never had growing up. "You have no idea how lucky you are," she would say, raising one nostril and glaring down at me with contempt. "It must be nice to have the option to be happy, to leave for school every day and not have to feel any pain at all. You have no idea what's it's like to be *me*." I knew better than to tell her that there was no escape from the misery I felt, or that she haunted my thoughts no matter where I was. My disguise had apparently worked on mom, too, if she actually thought I was lucky.

I didn't recognize it as jealously at the time. I just knew she hated me. Mom and I were no longer teammates or co-conspirators. I became a safe target for her anger and pain because I couldn't retaliate, and—more importantly—I couldn't leave her.

"Oh, I'm Melissa and my life is so great," she mocked. "My mom's, like, this total bitch, but I'm perfect, so that's all that matters. I don't care about anyone but myself." She completed her impression of me by prancing and waving her hands around. She reveled in my humiliation as my jaw and fists clenched. I wanted to punch her.

I had tried to be the one thing she didn't have to worry about. She didn't have to concern herself with my grades or behavior at school or wonder why I didn't have any friends. Instead of being grateful that she had a good kid, she hated me for it. I couldn't win, and I sure didn't feel very lucky.

"Asshole!" Mom screamed into the dead receiver. She slammed the phone down after he hung up on her and grabbed her coat and keys. "I'm going over there!" she said to no one in particular. My grandmother and I tried to stop her, but she got into her car and sped away to my dad's new house.

Dad had a girlfriend, and I knew mom was about to find out. She was already spiraling downward, and this would put her over the edge. I called my mom's friend, Pam, and she rushed over. I thought about calling my dad and warning him, but I knew he wouldn't pick up the phone. Talking to me made him feel guilty, so he rarely returned my calls. Despite what mom believed, I *had* lost my father.

The four of us sat in the living room and awaited mom's return, unsure of what her state of mind would be. We didn't have to wait long. Her car tore into the driveway so fast, I thought she might drive through the garage door. The squeal of her brakes brought us to our feet. I grabbed Aaron and unsuccessfully tried to distract him with a game.

"Did you know?" she hollered as she burst in the backdoor, her eyes wild and angry. "You all knew and let me make a fool of myself!" she accused between gasps of air. Pam and Grandma attempted to calm her, but I just stood there, frozen by her hysteria.

"She knew!" Mom screamed, pointing at me. "My own daughter! That little bitch knew and didn't tell me!" Fear seized my heart and tears hesitated behind my eyes, too afraid to make an appearance. My grandmother admonished her own daughter in my defense. "Do not talk to her like that, Lori Ann! This is not her fault." Grandma's words fell on deaf ears. My mother's wrath had found its convenient target.

Mom's behavior became more erratic as her therapy transitioned from discussing her divorce to diving into her past. As she worked through the traumas of being molested as a child, raped as a teenager and abused as a young wife by her first husband, her condition worsened. Her once secret, muffled whimpers evolved into deafening wails from which she no longer attempted to shield us. My mother had turned to glass and would shatter at the slightest touch. I tiptoed around her and handled her gently, more to protect myself than her.

Friends and family frequently came over to check on us, and my grandmother slept on our couch most of the week. Our pastor and his wife were often called in during mom's especially bad episodes. She could no longer function as a mother. She could be nothing but sad.

Our late night conversations were no longer about how much she loved/hated dad. Instead, mom held me hostage while she sobbed about all the emotional, physical and sexual abuse she had suffered throughout her life, at the hands of one man after another. I listened without visible emotion. I had become the rock of the family, and I could not fall apart as mom unraveled in front of me. I had always been afraid mom would ultimately hurt Aaron or me during one of her one of her fits of rage, but now I feared she would hurt herself.

Therapist Greg, whom I had started seeing as well, assured me that this was a normal part of therapy. He explained that mom had to hit the bottom of the pit, but that as she worked her way out, she would fill the pit up behind her so she wouldn't fall as deep each time. It would get worse before it got better, he said, but it would eventually get better. "You're lucky," he told me during what I didn't know would be our last session. "She's going through the phases of grief quickly, so you can expect her to improve real soon."

His words gave me little peace as mom's episodes intensified and her mental state became more and more fragile. Her insurance stopped covering our counseling, so Therapist Greg dropped us. The news shook my mother. "I'll *die* without him!" She had said the same thing about dad, except this time I thought maybe she was right.

"She's dead in there," I thought. Our mother's cries had quieted a while ago. I was sure that she had done it this time. I could feel her absence from the earth in my bones. The autumn day had already warmed up, and I could tell our Indian summer would last a little longer. Aaron and I played outside in our pajamas, the wet grass licking our bare feet. I fought back tears as I imagined where I would find her body and how I would protect my brother from seeing it.

Would she be dead on the bathroom floor or in the bedroom? Did she take a fistful of pills or would there be blood? Did she write a note? Would her last words be full of love for my brother and me, or full of hate for the world that had turned its back on her?

"We'll have to go live with Dad," I murmured. I wasn't sure which of us would be less excited about that. In that moment, I hated her for leaving us. I hated her for her selfishness, for only seeing her own pain, for being made of glass, for making me the rock, for handing us a life without our mother.

I looked at my brother, who only pretended that playing outside in our pajamas was a normal Saturday morning. Would he remember her? I wondered what I would say when he got older and asked about her. Maybe I'd tell him what a kind, gentle person our mother was and how much she loved us. I could paint for him the picture of what everyone wants their mother to be. Maybe he would never have to know the truth, and he could be the lucky one. Someone in this situation deserved to be the lucky one.

As I approached the backdoor, I practiced how I would explain our mother's death to Aaron in my head. I asked him to wait outside for just a minute and told him I would be right back. He stopped his play and sat on the step, afraid to be alone, but somehow knowing that he needed to be brave.

I walked through the empty rooms, pausing at each corner to prepare myself for the scene that might lay before me. I reached the hallway and peeked into the dark bathroom. Nothing. I stared at her closed bedroom door, remembering that I had left it open. My palms were damp as I slowly turned the knob.

I found my mother tucked into her bed, her head nestled on her pillow, her mouth agape. She snored slightly as she inhaled. She was absent from the earth, but she was still breathing.

I quietly backed out of the room and let her sleep.

Dras, Ras eir Irlan

fiction by
Jennifer M. Dillon

When time began and the orb of Ailanthea was just forming in the void still dark and lifeless, Raislaine rose and wandered trying to grasp the world with blind fingers. She felt the edges of shifting rock and slid on gravel ground. She walked mountains rising into the dark and through basins empty, waiting for water. Night after night she walked, wondering why she was alone in this place, her tears falling, wetting the ground. Eventually she walked the whole world and knew not what to do other than to walk it again. This time with her goddess-blessed fingers she felt the tiny beginnings of life. She tried to tend to these fragile beings but it was too cold for them to thrive and too dark for her to see and so without meaning to, she crushed them beneath her feet.

So she imagined the opposite of dark; she saw colors and plants, water and land, and willed new children for Ailanthea. Children nurturing the world, growing as it grew, dancing and warm. She lit the sun so she could see her way and warm those born from her loneliness. Those whose lives she made long. But Raislaine was not the only goddess born when the world formed.

Though they had missed each other in their beginnings, Drasbaine too had awoken and borne children, cradled and loved in the darkness, but they too were cold and didn't thrive as quickly or live as long as Raislaine's sun-warmed. Jealous, Drasbaine stole their life at night, pulling it from their dreams in threads that she wove into blankets to wrap her own children in.

Then Raislaine raised the first moon to drive the dark back, but it was not enough and she raised the second, but even still Drasbaine's nimble fingers pulled and wove. Finally, she raised the third moon driving the dark away from all of Ailanthea. But Drasbaine's children, now adapted to the cold, dark shadows began to die. Drasbaine's mother-heart was so broken and her tears so bitter that Raislaine took pity and said, "Cease your dream weaving and I will pull the moons and the sun from the skies for five days of each month. These days for you and yours. This I promise from one mother to another."

Drasbaine, the Mother of Dark and all that live in the shadows, took this bargain and taught her children the ways of patience and cunning. Though Raislaine's children's lives were shorter because of the bargain struck, they remained long still and during the darkspan they stayed inside, knowing these days belonged to Drasbaine and her brood.

Raislaine carved stairs to the top of the highest mountain where the sun always shone, except during the darkspan, and built her sanctuary. She built a home of light and cloud, of archways and wooden floors, gauzy curtains and light smooth silks. Drasbaine, in turn, built the Gate and the Shadow Keep within. A truce ruled the planet.

Raislaine awoke one night with a deep and hollow ache in her chest. Confused by this new feeling, she rose to walk until sleep invited her once again into his embrace. She walked across the blue grass fields to the edge of the wild woods and she was so deep in thought, she didn't notice the dirt path give away to obsidian tiles, or the wild trees to evenly-spaced ones.

Not until she heard tinkling and saw flashes made of neither light nor dark did she realize herself lost. The tinkling rang again, this time accompanied by a deep cry and Raislaine rushed to see who was being accosted. Stepping from the path and sliding through the evenly-spaced trees she veiled herself in their shadows until she came upon a clearing in which stood a man and a woman. Raislaine knew that they were not like her or the children of Ailanthea; she had wandered far indeed.

"Amuse me Irlan; tell me a tale, dash a dance, sing a sweet song," demanded the woman-shaped creature.

The woman too was of neither dark nor light, but all the beauty in between like lightning in a thundercloud. Her skin was silver and tarnish and along her limbs swirled eddies of energy. Her eyes were liquid pools of iridescence, no pupil or iris, and they shone with the beauty of powerful cruelty.

"A man can only know so many things, my Queen, and I fear that we have exhausted my repertoire," said Irlan.

"But you are not really a man, nor I a Queen," she sulked.

"You are so much more, Raelin," he said.

Raelin's face twisted into a snarl and she launched herself at Irlan who was bound at wrist, waist and ankle with the prettiest of shackles and wrapped her legs around him, raking his face with razor nails and nipping his neck with bladed teeth, riding him until she was bored once again.

"Come up with more amusement or suffer my idea of entertainment," she hissed before stalking from the clearing.

Though Raislaine knew not how she came to this place or even where she was, she knew she had to save him for when she looked at him the deep, hollow ache in her chest filled to the brim.

"You should leave, Lady of the Light, here you shine far too bright," said Irlan.

"Why does she treat you so?" asked Raislaine stepping to him.

"She cannot help what she is. She is of Maelrin. Existing where light and dark cannot claim."

"I would free you," said Raislaine.

"Then it seems my luck walks with you." And seeing Raislaine's confusion he said, "I would have you free me too."

Raislaine laid her hands on the chains and melted them away with a brush of pure *ras vere*. Once free, Irlan took her hand in his, bringing it to his lips and when she felt them she came alive from her fingertips to her crown.

"Come now, we must go. You know the way?"

"I do not even where we are, and can only remember part of the way back. I think I was dreaming when I came here," admitted Raislaine.

With fingers twined they ran through the evenly-spaced trees and back to the avenue of obsidian tiles and then raced along the slick ground even as the silver mists closed in on them, chased by Raelin, her howl shredding the air.

Finally, after their legs were past burning and they stumbled numb: "Leave me; I will survive here, but you will not," said Irlan shoving Raislaine away.

"No! We two are stronger as one," said Raislaine as she gathered the last of her *vere*, imbuing Irlan with it, lightening his step and strengthening his will.

Finally, they burst through the mists into the field of blue grass. Once their breathing calmed and their legs were ready to bear them again, Raislaine led Irlan up the carved stairs to the peak where she made her home. There they learned about love and tenderness, the heat of passion and laughter, until Drasbaine came.

As the moons slid into their places darkening Ailanthea, Raislaine could hear both the sighs of her children as they readied themselves for the cycle without the light and the gleeful giggles of the Dras brood they got ready to take over the surface for their days of freedom. Even though these sounds were the true music of Ailanthea, Raislaine's heart still ached for the sadness of her little ones. Irlan thought this Lady of the Light most beautiful even when dimmed by melancholy and came behind her, sliding his arms around her waist, and leaning his cheek against the hair that was always warm. He knew there were no words to soothe Raislaine's heart.

"It seems your fate Irlan to be found in the arms of one Mistress or another," said Drasbaine with a voice of smoke and brass. "Too bad that none seem strong enough to protect you from the next."

Raislaine turned at the sound of her sister goddess's voice. Drasbaine stood in the doorway, filling it with all the beauty that lives in the ebony of the night. The velvet darkness swirled and flowed around Drasbaine, both protecting and revealing, and in it Raislaine could see several of the Dras brood shining with love for their mother and something else not quite right.

"What is wrong with your children?" asked Raislaine.

"I do not know, but only he can help," said Drasbaine, her voice softened by Raislaine's concern.

The certainty in Drasbaine's voice gave Raislaine pause, and in her deepest heart she didn't want Irlan to go, especially now in the deep days of the darkspan but she knew too that she would never deny Drasbaine aid.

Irlan turned Raislaine to him and said, "I'll not be gone long my little Ras; I promise that I will return to you," sealing the promise with a kiss.

Raislaine watched Irlan take Drasbaine's hand and as Drasbaine pulled him through the Gate to the Shadow Keep, Drasbaine whispered across the distance, "Thank you; I will not forget this."

Irlan tried to take a step in the darkness and stumbled to his knees, unable to see through burning eyes.

Drasbaine caught him by the elbow and helped him back to his feet. "Easy Irlan. You are ras-blinded. Close your eyes."

Irlan did and soon felt Drasbaine's cool breath against his eyelids filling his feverish eye sockets and rolling down his checks, lips, and chin, chilling his skin so that it tingled, not entirely unpleasantly.

"Try now," said Drasbaine.

And Irlan slowly opened his eyes and saw the glory of the Shadow Keep. Vere-powered lights hung from the ceiling in various shapes and sizes, the onyx and hematite floors were covered with thick carpets. Large windows allowed Irlan to see the purple streaked sky filled with the winged of the Dras brood, some of which were playing and others of which were flying in formation. He heard the clash of weapons and saw flashes of *dras vere*.

"You are preparing for battle!" Irlan accused.

Drasbaine held up a hand to silence him. "Come."

She led him up a staircase to a room housing the afflicted Dras brood. Irlan walked among them, disturbed by what he saw. He came to a young broodling who was laid out on her side, and her wings stretched out behind her were eaten through in several places. Left behind was only a sheer sticky membrane.

"I thought it an infection sent by Raislaine, because only *ras vere* can destroy *dras vere* this thoroughly," said Drasbaine.

"Until you realized that it was too slow for that," said Irlan.

"Just so. If she was coming, she would just wipe us out with one cleansing sweep."

"And?" prodded Irlan.

"And her word has been good. I have no reason to doubt her."

"This isn't destroying your brood; it's changing them."

This startled and angered Drasbaine. "What do you mean changing?"

"Are these the first ones infected?" asked Irlan.

She shook her head and led him to a smaller room filled with the silence of the nearly dead. And she gasped, the bodies of her children were cocooned with the membrane and underneath the sticky layers their hearts could be seen beating still.

Drasbaine's roar of rage cracked stone and glass. She hovered over her children, dark tears burning holes in the membrane over their hearts. Then she reached and pulled from their chests their still beating hearts, consuming them, taking into herself all that was left of her poor corrupted children. When the last heart was gone, she raised her faceted eyes filled with pain and hatred to Irlan. "Who dares defile my children?"

Though he knew that this was the moment that would change Ailanthea forever he did the only thing that he could and answered the grieving mother. "Raeli of the Maelrin did this."

"Why?"

"Because I left her."

"For Raislaine, and yet it is my children who suffer for it!" Drasbaine growled large and terrible, raising wails among the sick.

"Your realm is easier for her to traverse than Raislaine's. But even this is not supposed to be possible. This is not the order of things," said Irlan, his voice growing and shifting like boulders on a mountain.

"How do you know this?" demanded Drasbaine.

With a heavy heart, knowing that his time on Ailanthea was done, and his promise to Raislaine broken, he split his mortal flesh stepping forth in his true form. Drasbaine flinched, trying to hold herself together in the vastness that was Irlan. Though he was still shaped like a man, his body was the void pierced with flashes of darker light. Around his head were clouds of colored gases in which small explosions could be seen and it was obvious that even this containment wasn't his natural state of being.

He showed her that he was of the universe itself, without him life doesn't form or spark; he brings substance forth from the void—he and the others like him.

"I am Irlan. And I know because I bring order to chaos. I will go and undo what I have done," and with eyes filled with deep sorrow and loss asked: "Will you tell her that I never meant to leave and that I will endeavor to keep my promise to her?"

"I will."

And then Irlan was gone, returned to the vast spaces between suns.

Drasbaine went to Raislaine and told her all that happened in the Shadow Keep. Raislaine asked not one question nor for a single explanation and when Drasbaine was done with her telling, she left Raislaine standing with her face turned up to the lightening sky.

Though her heart was breaking Raislaine knew that there were things larger in the universe than even a goddess born, and she knew too that she was lucky to have known his love at all. From that darkspan on, and for all that followed, when she looked at the stars she knew he was out there and part of her waits for him still.

Lucksmith

fiction by

Thomas Marlowe

It happened one winter that a certain Thorstein came to Vorz. He told them of the strait he was in; how the Berserker, who was called Asgaut, had challenged him to the holmgang (duel to the death)... that Asgaut had killed many of his people, and that he must give up his sister to him if they would not support him; for, said he, I have no confidence in the result of the holmgang, unless I have the benefit of the good luck which attends you.

- Viga Glum's <u>Saga</u>

"Not exactly your lucky day, eh?" said the ghost. Since I was at this point lying on my back in a dark room with a pile of rubble pinning me to the ground, dust in the air, and an alarming smell of smoke from somewhere not far enough away, I could only agree. I wasn't in pain and didn't think anything was broken, but I'd already tried to shift the big chunk of building material that was holding me in place and I couldn't. I'd tried shoving it off and squirming out from beneath it but all to no avail and it was about the time I realised I was stuck there that the ghost had turned up.

I assumed it was a ghost. It was transparent enough that I could see scenery through it, especially around the edges. Otherwise it was not what I expected a ghost to look like: an unkempt middle-aged man with scruffy dark hair turning to grey, a couple of days' worth of stubble, and a narrow and lined face. Also it was wearing an old suit with an overcoat. And it had a Scottish accent, but I suppose the Scots are entitled to come back as ghosts if they want.

"I don't have lucky days," I said, and I meant it.

"Now that surprises me," the ghost said and pointed a finger at me accusingly. "Are you sure about that?"

I glared at it. "Pretty sure yes," I said, "And, sorry, why would a ghost be turning up to challenge my own views on my own life?"

"What makes you think I'm a ghost, son?" He paused. "Ah, the whole see-through thing. Aye, well. Don't go jumping to conclusions, eh? You injured?"

It dawned on me that I was feeling remarkably calm about my predicament. The building had collapsed around me; I was trapped, there may well be a fire raging somewhere nearby, and I was talking to a picky Caledonian spectre, but I wasn't panicking. The weirdness of that realisation almost panicked me. "No, I don't think so. Can't move though. I don't suppose you can poltergeist this stuff off me could you?"

"Firstly, I'm not a ghost," the ghost said, "Secondly 'poltergeist' is not a verb. And no, I can't.

I'm not even here. I'm currently about a quarter mile in that direction and looking about as *compos-mentis* as an English tourist on his first trip to Amsterdam. You know, all overawed by tulips and Anne Frank."

"Am I hallucinating?" This seemed a reasonable question in the face of this insanity. The ghost just snorted.

"If your subconscious dredges me up in times of stress then you ought to get that seen to," he said. "Anyway, let's stick to the matter at hand, eh? Help is on its way and with any luck help will arrive before the other side does. But there's not a lot we can do about that, so let's do the polite shall we? My name's Lucas; what's yours?"

"Danny," I said. "Hansen. Wait, what do you mean 'the other side'? The other side as in 'beyond the veil' or the other side as in—"

"As in the bad guys, Danny," said Lucas. "As in the enemy. Your enemy and mine. And they're on their way. Who did you think blew up the building, son?"

After a few seconds of silence I realise my mouth had fallen open and that I was staring at the ghost—Lucas—with an expression that would have made a goldfish tell me to stop looking so gormless. I closed my mouth, swallowed and took another second or two to gather my thoughts.

"Blew it up?" I asked in a strained voice. I barely remembered the last few moments before everything came crashing down. I'd been on my way to meet my friend Alex and then... I'd heard his voice from inside an open door and... "What happened?"

Lucas thrust his hands in the pockets of his overcoat as though looking for something in there. "You were lured into an empty office building Danny. They messed with your mind and lured you in, one of their Siren tricks probably. Did you see a naked woman, hear a distressed child crying for help, long lost relative calling your name?"

"My friend Alex," I said, "just saying hello."

"Lord above. Seriously, your subconscious needs to get out more. Anyway. Siren. Lure. Boom."

"A bomb? Someone bombed a building just to kill me? Why... who...?" I tried to stop babbling but it was a struggle. I felt entitled to a little babble.

"Bomb? No, nothing of the sort, they kind of... poltergeisted it down on you." He grinned. "And as for 'who' we haven't got time for that right now. Like I said, they're probably on their way to finish the job. My side's on their way too, but they're having to do it the hard way, finding their way through the rubble and the fire."

"Fire? Crap..." I'd smelled the smoke but it was only now that the reality of what that meant hit me. I started to struggle again under the rubble, pushing at it with my hands, feeling the sharp edges cut into my palms. I tried to wriggle my hips free, but the weight on them was too much. The ghost stepped forward.

"Hey, hey," he said. "Don't panic, just... I'm trying to keep you calm, son; it will help, but you need to work with me, okay?"

I tried not to panic. Something Lucas had said suddenly made things make more sense. "You're keeping me calm? Really? I wondered why I wasn't bloody terrified. You're messing with my head?"

"Oh, aye," Lucas said happily. "Anyway. Help's on its way. Let's talk about something else. Let's talk about luck. Are you a lucky man, Danny?"

My immediate response was a denial couched in colourful and earthy metaphors that made Lucas grin wickedly.

"So you're not then?" he said, summarising my response rather more politely. "Tell me about it."

So I told him. Just the recent highlights.

Until a month ago I had a decent job. It wasn't much but it suited me. I could turn up just before nine in the morning and make phone calls to other businesses in the hope that they would be thrilled to buy office supplies from me. The pay was worthwhile, the work was easy and I could browse the Internet. Then one Friday afternoon the boss gathered us together with some excellent news.

"We've had a brilliant year," he told us, "and I'm happy to tell you that our success is leading to bigger things and some exciting opportunities."

The bigger thing was being bought by one of our rivals. The exciting opportunity was the chance to relocate a hundred miles away. At least that was the chance for the three members of staff that the new owners wanted to keep on the books. I was not one of them.

Until a month ago I had a girlfriend. She was named Leia, after the character from *Star Wars* and she'd never forgiven her parents for that. Leia was fun to be around and had a great sense of humour as long as you stayed clear of science fiction. We had some good times, watched a lot of serious movies, and then she decided she couldn't live without the affectionate presence in her life of my former best friend Kevin, who was a fan of *Star Trek* and was taking an online course in Klingon. Kevin was over the moon and the last I saw of them they were discussing where to buy a beehive wig to complete a Janice Rand cos-play outfit.

Until a month ago I had a place of my own. Just a bedsit above a takeaway but it was mine. A couple of rooms, a decent bed, a shower that worked more often than not and a ready supply of curry and rice for when culinary inspiration failed me. It was handy for the buses too, just a couple of streets away from the station which meant that getting to work and back was never a problem. When I had a job. But then Mister Gopal got a cash offer from the pizza shop at the other end of the block and sold the takeaway and the bedsit to "Call me Harry" the Turkish guy that ran the pizza shop, and "Call me Harry" explained that he was planning to turn the bedsit into storage for one of his other businesses (probably the counterfeit DVD distribution business providing all the local area's cut price blockbusters and dodgy Czechoslovakian porn requirements).

Lucas chuckled at that. "So what have you been doing since?"

"Borrowing a couch off my friend Alex," I replied. "Though that's likely to change."

"Because you're trapped under a pile of rubble in a burning building?" Lucas asked.

I swore again at the recollection. "Well, yes, probably. But also he's got himself a girlfriend all of a sudden. Wasn't even trying. And now he wants his apartment to himself. Or at least free of me."

Lucas seemed unduly interested in Alex's love life. He squatted down near me. "Tell me about this new girlfriend."

"What? I don't know; I haven't met her yet. He only met her yesterday, came home full of himself and telling the story. He was late out of the house yesterday, his alarm clock didn't go off, so he caught the bus after the one he normally gets. Turns out there was only one seat, and it was next to this girl, and she was reading a book he's just finished reading so they got talking and... and why am I talking about Alex's new bloody girlfriend with a Scottish ghost?"

"I'm not a ghost," said Lucas. "I told you." He stood up and popped a throat lozenge in his mouth, having finally retrieved it from his coat pocket. "You know what I think, Danny Hansen? I think you're a very lucky man indeed."

I think I probably swore again. I may have made unflattering references to Scotland. I certainly expressed my disagreement with him in vehement and picturesque terms.

"Swearing doesn't impress me, Danny," Lucas said. "I'm from Glasgow. Seriously I've heard nuns swear better than that at preschoolers. I mean it though. You're a lucky man. Just not for yourself. I wasn't expecting that, not that specifically, but that's why I'm here. I was sent to find you."

I didn't answer but he could tell he had my undivided attention, so he went on.

"I can't do the whole story now, son," he said, "but there's a war on. A big war. The biggest. Good versus evil, all that bollocks. My side doesn't like using simplistic language like that, but time's short. I'm working for the good guys, though I suppose everyone thinks that, eh? And I was sent to find someone special that we'd really, really like to be on our side. And that, Danny Hansen, is you."

I was starting to feel short of breath and light-headed. I opened my mouth to speak but nothing came out. Lucas kneeled beside me and put his hand on my forehead. I could feel his hand there, transparent though he was.

"They're getting through," he said, "the other side. They've found you. I'll try to keep the bastards out as long as I can. Listen to me Danny, keep listening to me, eh? I'll tell you the rest and you stay with me to listen."

It seemed important to him to do as he said, and the rest of the room was fading away anyway. I listened and tried not to shatter into pieces with the pressure building in my head.

"The old Norse people believed that luck was a real force," Lucas said, "part of a man's soul. They called it the *hamingja*. Some people had a very powerful one, and things went their way. They got all the breaks, all the luck. In battle, in love, in those contests where they throw axes at the braids of those busty viking lasses too, I suppose. I saw that in a film, might not have happened. Anyway, some people had a powerful *hamingja* and you know what? Those people were sought after. Aye."

His voice was all I knew now, his voice and the touch of his hand on my forehead. Everything else was cold blackness and crushing pressure, and the desire (oh the desire) to just give in, give up and go under. But his voice and his hand kept me here.

"It's all in the sagas, Danny," he went on. "If there was an important battle, or a dangerous expedition, they'd go in search of someone who was powerfully lucky and try to get them to come along. Sometimes they didn't even have to come along in person; they could send their *hamingja* along regardless and their good luck would work for the other people. And you know what, Danny Hansen; when you told me your little life story just now it stood out like a cockney at a ceilidh. Everyone around you has had an awful lot of lucky breaks. Your boss, your girlfriend and your old best buddy, your landlord. Your flatmate. Everyone but you. Hold on a second; I think I can push them back."

My head hurt suddenly but the room was back, and the cold darkness had gone along with the desire for blissful oblivion. Lucas was looking tired as though he'd been working hard, and I suspected that he had being doing just that on my behalf. A war, he'd said, and I guessed that he'd been fighting it somehow right there and then.

"So...I'm kind of a rabbit's foot?" I said, "A lucky charm for everyone but me?"

Lucas nodded. "Aye, I suppose so. I didn't expect that. I was sent to find this man with a powerful *hamingja* to get him to join our team. I was expecting some good-looking flash bastard with winning lottery tickets hanging out of every pocket and a couple of supermodel girlfriends with perfect bodies and no sense of self-esteem at all. Instead..."

"Me."

"Aye, you. But tell you what, son, our side could really use that sort of luck working for us. This war... well it's not going well. And we could use every little edge we can get."

Insanity. "This war... why haven't I heard of it? Where is it being fought?"

"Everywhere," Lucas said. "Everywhen. I'll not lie to you Danny Hansen, if you say yes, if you join us, there may be times you wish I'd left you here in this room. For the flames. For *them*."

Well that was a point well made, wasn't it? "And is that what you'll do if I say 'no'?" I said, "I either join you or you leave me here?"

Lucas shrugged. "That's a very stark way of putting it, son," he said, "We'd do our best to get you out, but... well... the odds are against it. The building's in a bad way and my people are having trouble reaching you. And *they*—the enemy—have a lot of power brought to bear on this place to find you, and us, and make sure nothing leaves the place alive. We'd do our best to get you out safely, even if you say no, but to be honest..." And here he grinned the sort of grin that always made me want to slap my older brother when he played me at chess and saw I'd walked right into his trap again, "...without a lot of luck on our side we don't stand a chance."

"And the only way you'd be that lucky," I said coldly, "is if I was on your side?"

Lucas opened his eyes in theatrical realisation.

"My God, I think you may have something there," he said. "So what do you say?"

"Just call me Rabbit's Foot," I said and reached out a hand, feeling he and I should shake on the deal. He took it and I felt a cold pressure that was not entirely solid. At the same moment the wall to the right of me crumbled and bowed outward a little and the light of a powerful torch shone in and onto me, dazzling me.

"About bloody time," Lucas said and I assumed that the new arrivals were on his team...our team... "Get this crap off our new recruit, will you, and let's get out of here before they send a whole bloody hive after us."

One of the newcomers, a burly man in combat fatigues, started manhandling the rubble off me with alarming ease. The other, a teenage girl with bright red dreadlocks, knelt by me and grinned. "New recruit are you?" she said, her accent upper class and cultured. "Bad luck for you."

"Seems that way," I said feeling the weight move off my lower body and started to shuffle myself backward.

"Welcome aboard, Lucksmith," she said and gave me her hand to help me up. "Welcome to the war."

Thirteen

fiction by

Kelly Kohles

Smoke. Black. Thick. My earliest memory.

I was three when it ripped me awake and twisted around me, a dark blanket trying to lure me back to sleep. Pops and hisses whispered from another room.

Terror sliced through me and all I wanted was to chase the darkness away.

I scrambled away from the black as it poured under the door, falling out of bed. The white bunny lamp I always left on was dark. I pushed the button with such force I knocked it to the floor. The shade fell off the lamp, taking the bulb and the bunny's head with it.

I screamed.

Smoke swirled into my throat and the coughing began. I dropped to the floor again, my hands striking something sharp.

I was on all fours—coughing—when light filled my open window. It was so bright I turned away to shield myself, then almost screamed again when a pair of brown eyes, wide and scared, met my own.

There was relief over having light, at discovering my baby sister and not the monster of my dreams.

It was replaced by anger, seeing her clutching Anna, the rag doll that reigned as my most prized possession.

I forgot all else and tried to yank Anna from Jenny's arms. With each pull Jenny slid closer to me until a sickening rip sliced through the hisses and crackles. Anna's arm dangled from my fingers. Tears, hot and heavy, ran down my cheeks as rage consumed me.

The magical light still lit my room and I saw the bottom of my lamp. Without thinking, I picked it up, ready to throw it at my sister.

The house chose that moment to groan—a dying breath before a thundering crash rolled into the room. A wave of heat followed, reminding me of an open oven.

The lamp slid out of my hands, but I never heard it drop—the crackling noise too loud. The smoke thickened, trying to steal the light.

"Get out!" The voice was gravel laced with sugar—just like Granddad.

I ran to the light but couldn't climb out—my chin only reached the bottom of the windowsill.

I was coughing again. My eyes burned and my chest was tight.

"Pretend it's a cookie," the voice said.

Sweat covered my body as I scanned the room for something to stand on.

I crawled toward an old folding chair by the door—my actions controlled by my fear of the absolute darkness above me. The heat pulsed around me and I wondered if I'd burst into flames.

I touched the chair and it burned. I screamed again, the smoke following my cries as I inhaled and the coughs hit me again.

I couldn't breathe.

The white light was gone, transformed into a blinking red.

I crawled toward my bed and Jenny, left where I'd tugged her. I collapsed next to her, my strength gone. A warm glow bathed her peaceful face, sleeping, the remnants of Anna still clutched in her arms.

I reached to grab Anna away only to find myself floating away from them.

"Anna!" I screamed, my hands reaching for my doll as the distance increased.

My eyes drooped, gritty and watery. I heard voices and continued to fly, cold air hitting my skin. I could see light beneath my eyelids and knew the darkness was at bay.

And I slept.

It was November 13, 1970.

Friday the thirteenth.

"You got the devil inside you, child." Aunt Patty always followed her declaration by quickly performing the sign of the cross. What followed varied depending on what I was accused of.

Not doing my chores? Five smacks with the ruler onto the burn scars seared into my hands. The reason Uncle Jim drank too much? The broom closet for an hour.

If I dared cry or speak, she sent me to her favorite place: the storm shelter.

The first time Aunt Patty put me there I screamed myself hoarse and couldn't speak for a week.

I learned to be quiet.

"I always told your momma you'd be the death of her. I knowed from the day you was born you was cursed. I told her to give you up but she didn't listen to me." It was her second favorite litany, signaling a whooping with the paddle. "I got to beat the evil out of you, child," she said, her syrupy voice making each sting worse.

Jenny always watched, holding the most beautiful porcelain doll—the hospital had tossed Anna with our clothes—and sucking her thumb. She hadn't spoken since the fire.

I didn't want to hate Jenny. She still escaped her bed and sought mine—the nights I didn't sleep in the shelter. She snuggled next to me while I pretended she was Anna, stroking the blond curls from her forehead and humming a song I didn't remember learning.

Aunt Patty discovered us one morning, her pale skin so mottled with rage she reminded me of a fat purple grape.

My bed became the cellar during the cold months, but as soon as spring hit Aunt Patty moved me to the storm shelter. "I won't have no evil sleeping in this house!"

Jenny and I were separated. I spent the warm days running about the farm trying to avoid my aunt while Jenny remained indoors—too frail since the fire to do much more than sit and play with her doll. We only saw each other when storms hit, the four of us hiding in the shelter together.

Time moved, marked by the seasons. In winter I was allowed inside again, banished to the cellar.

The winter memories remain lost and I don't try to find them.

My birthday went uncelebrated until Aunt Patty sent me to school.

The day was hot and sticky and I hated the scratchy dress she tossed to me. The shoes were too tight and pinched my feet. I thought the teacher, Miss Mason, the most beautiful woman in the world. I can't remember her face anymore, only the musical lilt of her voice—as if each word belonged in a song—and how the scent of flowers followed her.

"We're going to go around the circle and each of you needs to tell me your name, how old you are, and your birthday," she sang. One by one each kid answered.

Then it was my turn and I sat silent, unsure of what to say. I didn't know the answers.

Miss Mason prodded me a few more times and I shrugged in response. "We'll talk later then," she said, letting the others finish.

At lunch the other kids pulled out boxes of food or got into line for trays. Not having a box I followed the other kids, only to be turned away without a ticket. My stomach growled as I sat down.

"Where's your food?" the boy I sat next to asked. I shrugged, again not knowing the answer.

"Are you stupid? Why don't you talk?"

Miss Mason found me there, sitting stoically as the other kids laughed at me. She scolded them and pulled me away, bringing me back to the classroom. She unfolded her sandwich and gave me half. It was gone so quickly, the other half soon followed.

"Do you go by Sandra or Sandy?"

I shrugged. The names no longer seemed familiar.

She tried again. "What does your mother call you?"

"Momma's dead." The words, the first I'd spoken that day, were muffled by the sandwich.

"I'm so sorry, dear. Who takes care of you?"

"Aunt Patty."

She nodded. "And what does Aunt Patty call you?"

Evil. Satan's spawn. Cursed. "Child."

She frowned. "That won't do. We need something special to call you. What name do you like?"

"Anna." This answer I knew.

"How about I call you Sandra Anna?"

I nodded so hard Miss Mason laughed and I smiled.

She peered into her book. "It says here you turn six next month. On...October 13. I'll be sure to put it on my calendar so we can celebrate. Here's a note for Aunt Patty about getting you a lunch ticket."

The note brought me another paddling.

"Ungrateful child! You know food feeds the evil."

Aunt Patty sent me to school with a slice of bread. I ate it on the way.

Miss Mason shared her lunch with me again. The next day, she pressed a ticket into my hand and I had hot food for the first time in years.

I counted down to my birthday. I saw other kids have parties at school and craved one of my own.

The Friday arrived and I couldn't wait for Aunt Patty to unlock the storm shelter so I could go to school.

Time passed, my growling stomach measuring how breakfast had come and gone. My ears worked overtime in the darkness, trying to make out her footfalls and the sliding of the outside bar fastening the doors shut.

The faint drone of a tractor was the only noise.

Anger, hot and fresh, bubbled beneath my skin. It had slept, waiting until Miss Mason's kindness brought a dangerous gift: hope.

I imagined Aunt Patty dead and going to live with Miss Mason. I pictured Jenny standing outside the kitchen window while I ate hot food at the table, her doll at my side.

"I hate them!" I yelled into the shelter.

My anger exhausted me and I fell asleep. When I woke up the room was very dark, as if night had fallen. I listened, startled by the silence. No birds or motors. Not a whisper of wind and the crickets refused to chirp.

Fear took over, that the world was empty and I remained alone.

Then light flashed through the cracks, a low rumble answering from far away, and I knew why the air was still. I counted the flashes, certain the storm would bring the others to me and at last I'd be free.

Before this day, I welcomed storms. They were the one time I imagined us a family, huddled together in safety.

Only this time, I remained alone. I shivered as thunder shook the earth holding me captive. The wind knocked on the doors with such force I thought they'd break free. My ears popped and a train roared by, confusing me because the farm held no tracks. I heard wood groan and break, so like the sounds from the fire. I began screaming.

"Sleep," said a voice.

Then there was blackness and my mind slept.

A room full of children greeted me, each in their own bed. Christmas decorations adorned the walls. A woman in white gave me water. "The doctor will be here soon."

A man in a jacket arrived. He smelled like peppermint. "Do you remember your name?"

I nodded.

He smiled. "What is it?"

"Sandanna," I said, the word barely a croak.

He asked me more questions until my voice quit. I knew some answers were wrong because he frowned.

The hospital sent me to a special doctor. I was supposed to talk to him, but he smelled too much like Aunt Patty, of moth balls and stale cigarettes. All I wanted was the answer to one question.

"When can I go back to school?"

He refused to answer. He kept pestering me with questions like, "What's the last thing you remember?" and "How do you feel?"

Two could play his game. I didn't answer.

The hospital said I was healed and I waited for Aunt Patty to pick me up. Instead an old woman came, her hair pulled into such a tight bun I imagined her roots ripping out. Her skin was as gray as her hair, like she belonged in the black and white TV.

She drove me to a large house that matched her perfectly and told me this would be my home until a better one could be found.

I didn't ask about Aunt Patty, afraid I'd be sent back with her. I tried to fit in with the other kids my age, but they scattered whenever I tried to play with them.

"She's cursed," they whispered, as if Aunt Patty's disciples.

They sent me to school, a different one. We rode a huge yellow bus forever to get there. When I asked my new teacher where Miss Mason was she sent me to the principal's office.

He reminded me of Granddad—from his voice to the salt and pepper hair. I wanted to ask him if he was the one who talked to me but was afraid he'd send me away.

He brought in another lady, much younger. Together they told me what everyone had hidden from me.

Three months ago a tornado had hit in mid-afternoon, destroying my school and half the town. They didn't know what happened to Miss Mason.

It took weeks to get the courage to ask The Gray Lady about Jenny.

"Who, dear?"

I described Jenny as I'd last seen her—long wavy blonde hair with ribbons, carrying a porcelain doll. When I mentioned Jenny didn't speak, she smiled.

"She was your sister? She found a lovely foster family to live with. Poor dear, we couldn't find any records with her name on it. I'll have to let them know."

She questioned me about Jenny—what did Jenny like to eat, had she ever talked—but learned I knew little.

"Do you want us to find you a family together?"

"No." My answer came without hesitation.

Saint Valentine's Day was the next day, the significance lost to me until my seventh birthday.

We spoke of Jenny once more, two months later.

"She's being adopted. Isn't that wonderful?"

"Yes ma'am," I said, disappointed and relieved my sister was far from the anger building inside.

It was Friday, April 13.

My seventh birthday coincided with a festival the town held "to remember those lost" on the one year anniversary.

The day was sticky and warm as the bus brought us to the festivities. Carnival games and rides were scattered throughout, placed on slabs of concrete that once held buildings.

Each time I attempted to use the ride ticket The Gray Lady had given me, the kids made signs of the cross. They either fled the line or shoved me away.

I gave up and found my old school, parts of it still under construction. A plaque stood by the entrance but I couldn't read it.

"I was home sick that day." The boy stood next to me, a full head taller and a black circle around one eye. I didn't recognize him so I guessed he didn't live in the home.

"It was my birthday," I said.

"Yeah?"

"Miss Mason was going to give me a party, but my aunt didn't let me go."

"Lucky you."

I glared at him. "I missed my party. That's not lucky."

He shook his head at me. "You mean you don't know? She died with most of her class when a wall fell on them during the tornado. Your aunt saved your life."

Tears fell down my face right as the sky opened up.

It became known as The Day of the Flood.

Thomas remained the only kid willing to brave my "curse"—he's also the one who explained it to me.

"You're a Friday the 13 baby. You're a magnet for bad luck."

"Why aren't you scared?"

He shrugged. "You've only been good luck for me. I haven't had my lunch stolen in months."

Whether I intended it or not, everything important in my life happened on the thirteenth, both bad and good—often intertwined with one another.

Every potential foster family arrived on the thirteenth. Once the smoke alarm went off. Another time a water pipe burst. One couple was willing but became ill after a visit and I never saw them again.

Word spread and no one else tried.

The next time my birthday fell on a Friday I was eleven. I was eating breakfast when Granddad whispered "run" into my ear. I cut school and hid in a cornfield. The bus driving the kids to school blew a tire and rolled down an embankment. Four dead, twelve injured.

The Gray Lady blamed me and did everything she could to force me out. She died of a heart attack exactly six months later—another Friday.

My thirteenth birthday I was called into the principal's office. An old lady sat next to him.

"My wife and I want you to live with us," he said.

On June 13, 1980, Thomas and I snuck into a movie theater to see *Friday the 13th*. His hands were up my shirt half the movie but I refused to go any further for fear of being murdered if I went to pee.

Friday, February 13, 1981 a car struck Grandpa —he insisted I call him that—and he went to the hospital. While scanning for broken bones, they found a mass in his chest. Cancer.

They caught it early and I had fifteen more years with him.

Thomas didn't get my virginity until the blizzard on January 13, 1984. He was driving me home when it hit and we took shelter in a barn for two days.

I embraced my "curse"—I had "13" tattooed on my lower back. Thomas proposed and we were married in 1985—on September 13.

We laughed when the doctor gave us a due date of June 16. Our son arrived at 12:59 AM—the thirteenth hour—of June 13. We named him Mason.

Twenty-two years later, as I sliced a piece of cake on his birthday, a voice whispered again.

"Look."

The last of my resentment slid away. I hired a private investigator to find Jenny and waited. Five years.

Today is my 28th wedding anniversary and I'm shaking with the news: Jenny's name is Anna now. She lives a three hour drive away.

I pick up the phone and wonder if she remembers.

A Man With A Satisfied Mind

fiction by

Andra L. Watkins

I knew I put that blasted still around there someplace. Noted for the future: it was a bad idea to sample my different batches before I drew up my map. It fortified me for the trek out there, though, to the bullseye at the center of nowhere.

My flask gave me extra doses of courage to face the quiet. The stillness. It was a backdrop for thousands of shifty things I never could make out. But they lurked there. Just beyond the line of trees and scrub. Over the lip of the next hill. Or the next.

I thrashed through a thicket. Climbed over some rocks. Next thing I knew, I fell. Through a hole in the earth. A tipsy speed demon in the dark.

I grabbed at flimsy roots and chawed on hands full of dirt. With a quick look at the fleeting pinhole of light, I vowed not to drink so much next time, if only the Eternal would give me a next time. Jagged rocks scraped the skin off my knuckles and tore at my work clothes.

The earth was eating me alive. I wondered if all the alcohol I consumed would give it heartburn, make it burp.

Those were my thoughts right before I landed hard on my rear end. Water trickled from the end of my nose, and when I looked up, I saw that I had fallen about twenty feet. All that drunken melodrama, for twenty measly feet into a well.

Only, when I looked around me, I was in more of a cavern. The rock floor was slick with sweat, and the faint light from above twinkled on the walls and ceiling, constellations underground. Cool air blew in my face from one direction or another.

Some old man once told me my land was like a buried sponge. Crannies and crevices, cracks and canyons that twisted and bore on forever.

I always thought he sampled too much of his own firewater, but as I crumpled my hat and set it alight with a dose of my own moonshine, I knew better. Behind the shadows that danced on the walls and licked the white button roof, I saw it again: that knowing look behind the whites of his eyes.

I shrieked and dropped my lantern, and it rolled over that brume all the way to the Old Man's bony feet. It was him. Something about the insides of his eye sockets was familiar, or maybe it was his gumless grin. Same two decayed teeth in there, a little worse for wear.

"I suppose you wonder how it is I got down here." He said it like it was completely logical for a skeleton to talk. Like I wouldn't shit my pants or have a come-to-Jesus moment with my moonshine.

Instead, I slid on the cave floor when I turned to run, and I fell and hit my head. Light pinwheeled through my eyes, and I was blind when it abated.

I heard the Old Man, though. Breathing. His breath whipped between his ribs and whistled through the triangle in his skull where his nose used to be.

Clearly, I have made an abominable batch of moonshine, because I am hallucinating.

While my hands and feet scrabbled to gain purchase on the floor, the Old Man who really wasn't there cackled and kicked my lantern along the floor.

"Might want to take that with you, if you're gonna find your way out of here. Since I never did."

I stared into the holes where his eyes once lived and imagined the yellowed orbs from when I knew him above. I gulped with enough vigor to make an echo. "How did you find this place, anyway?"

"Now, that is a secret, young man. Best not shared. But, there are other things I can show you. If you're interested."

He drummed his bony fingers along the wall, and my light flamed higher. Brighter. "I promise you, son. The light will last as long as you need. Unless you don't want to see."

With another thump of bones on the wall, my lantern blew out, and I met the darkness that had seen no light. I was engulfed by the blackness of hell. A total blindness, born without eyes.

I waved my hands in front of my face and felt the air rush over my skin. It was a suffocating pitch that made me gasp for breath. Even though I had plenty of oxygen, the walls of my crypt-like cocoon closed in. I pawed at my unseeing eyes and screamed, thinking sound alone might illumine my surroundings.

My voice retreated, and I was left with his bone-scraping melody along the wall. "Won't do no good to go and lose your mind, you know. You'll still die down here in the end. Like me."

"Maybe insanity will make it bearable." I rasped it through clenched teeth and tasted my own salty blood.

Another flick of his unseen white fingers, and my lantern was alight. It pulsed through the center of his skull and glowed within his socket eyes. "It won't." He whispered it. "Follow me."

We wound through a series of underground canyons. Chasms that wound into the earth forever. Sheer rock walls that led into the abyss. As I crawled along a foot-wide ledge behind him, I muttered, "Is this hell?"

"No." His voice shimmered in the dimness. "It is your salvation."

"Why does salvation seem like I'm damned?"

"Because," the Old Man replied, "you are too blind to see."

"I'm sorry?"

"It is your mission to bring people here. To hell. Or whatever this is." The Old Man's bones knocked together. The end of his finger fell into a sort of Grand Canyon underground, gobbled up by darkness. It pinged along rock ledges until I no longer heard it falling.

"I hope you didn't need that." I made my tone sympathetic.

"People will pay to see whether or not I can reclaim that piece of finger. Among other things."

"But, that means I have to get out of here. Alive."

The Old Man raked his knife-life fingers across dead space. "Enough. If I show you the way, will you bring people to this place? Will you show them the wonders of my grave?"

I smiled. "What does that mean, exactly? 'The wonders of your grave' might not attract a large audience as a tagline. Rather morbid, if you know what I mean."

He knocked his fingers against his chin. Nodded his empty head. "I see that. Yessssssss." It hissed through his gumless teeth. "So, you're alive. You tell me. How would you attract the living to a crypt?"

I took in the glittering rock walls. The gaping drop-off next to my feet. The labyrinth with underground rooms that soared to heaven and depths licked by the flames of hell. Level ground for a still, concealed from prying eyes.

"If I charged admission to this place, I'd have to have moonshine available for sale. And maybe firearms for target shooting. The reverberation of sound would drive people mad for the experience."

His spine creaked when he nodded. "Go on."

"They'd want to crawl along the ledges of these canyons like I did. With you. The possibility of death lingering at every humid turn. With complete darkness for just long enough to make them a little crazy."

"If I show you the way out, will you return? Create this underground empire in my honor? Will you do it?"

Could I make a living leading people through the dark?

I closed my eyes and shook what accounted for his hand. When he led me to a slit in the earth, I slid through it into the sunshine.

"Don't forget me," the Old Man whispered as I gulped fresh air and registered the scene around me. A fenced enclosure. A horse or two. My own land. When I squinted, sunlight caught the metal of my still, gleaming through the trees on the other side of the divide.

And so it was that I commenced the grand art of cave tour guide, taking paying customers through a crack in my own land. With the Old Man's help, we charted the biggest drop-offs, the darkest caverns, the yawning spaces with the mightiest echo for target practice, and the best spots for adult refreshment. It was an underground respite from the stuffy, judgmental world.

I led my charges crawling on hands and knees across foot-wide ledges with no barrier to break their falls. We used Chinese fireworks to light up the tightest spots. Some of the men challenged each other to duels of honor, their guns reverberating for hours around the buried rooms. We drank. We broke bottles, shot them to smithereens.

Sometimes, before the lights went out, I saw the Old Man, shimmering in the fringes, an elusive smile stretched across his skull. He left tokens, little pieces of the place for people to take as souvenirs of their visit to his grave. A rock. Some fur. A dried fish with no eyes. A startled bat.

I made more money underground than I did above it. In fact, I became a very rich man. It was several years before the Old Man extracted his payment, satisfaction for services rendered.

It was the last tour of the day. The Old Man came out to help me straighten up and extinguish the lights like he always did. And he took his spot along one wall while I poured myself one last jar of moonshine before I headed out into the starlit night. He watched me with those holes for eyes, scrutiny that no longer made me shiver or shake.

"How much do you reckon you've made in this place over the years?" He crossed one bony leg over the other while I filled my jar another inch.

"Just north of a half million. It was my lucky day, falling into that hole in the ground and finding you."

His teeth clattered together when he laughed. "No no no. I was the one who came out ahead. It was lonely down here all those years. It's been a pleasure to have the company."

I smiled and started to take another sip of my moonshine, but the sight of my hand stopped me. Outlines of bones glowed through my fading skin. I pushed up my sleeve and blinked as my flesh receded, and my fingers sounded hollow against the empty chamber of my skull.

When I looked at the Old Man again, I screamed at my own human likeness staring back at me with icy blue eyes and a hint of a smile.

"Thanks for helping me make my fortune. It was my lucky day, when you fell into that hole in the ground and found me. Enjoy your time underground."

And he extinguished the lights.

And he left me in a cave where I await the next unsuspecting lucky soul who comes my way.

Beauty From Ashes

memoir by

Jenny Cooper Rumble

Since my husband Jason and I began trying for a baby last year, I imagined in great detail what it would be like when we finally saw a positive pregnancy test. I pictured tears of joy followed by tight hugs and warm laughter. Jason, filled to the brim with excitement, would wrap me in his giant arms, lift me from the floor, and twirl me around in that strong yet gentle way he always did. The following months would lead to increased elation with each doctor visit and ultrasound. Jason would stand beside me, holding my hand at each appointment, unapologetically letting tears roll down his face as he watched our baby wiggle and dance. I envisioned him lovingly rubbing my growing belly through the months, placing gentle kisses on it, and cooing to his unborn child in his special brand of baby-talk that was somehow both ridiculous and charming. I couldn't wait for the day I could see him hold his child for the first time. Babies and children flocked to Jason like moths to a flame, and seeing him interact with them was always a fascinating and wonderful sight, bringing with it such heartwarming pride. I couldn't wait to see him as a father. What joys we would share as parents!

The day I saw a positive pregnancy test was nothing like what I had imagined. It was July 12, 2012, three weeks after Jason's funeral.

June 18th began like any other Monday, but ended like none I'd ever imagined. It was Jason's day off, so I woke up early and quietly went through my morning routine while he slept. Before leaving for work, I walked over to the bed to kiss him goodbye. It was then I discovered he wasn't breathing. Nineteen agonizing hours later, my twenty-nine-year-old husband was pronounced dead, and I found myself a young widow with absolutely no idea what to do next.

The next three weeks were blurry and numb. Blurry and numb were his services and burial. Blurry and numb were the days that followed as I busied myself with mundane tasks. Blurry and numb was the week I returned to my job. Blurry and numb were my days as they began to resemble a new life, a life without my love...a life I had never ever imagined.

On a Thursday in mid-July I bought a pregnancy test on a whim. The thought had crossed my mind a couple of times, but I had continually dismissed the possibility, refusing to take a test. I'm not sure why I put it off so long. Maybe it was dread of facing a negative result and mourning our children with a newer sense of finality. Perhaps it was fear that I could actually be carrying Jason's baby...the baby he'd never get to meet. Whatever the reason, I had put it off.

Moments later, I witnessed a second pink line appear on the test. Positive.

My head began to spin. My vision blurred. All I wanted to do was pace the floors of my house, but my legs behaved as if they'd forgotten how to operate. The feelings of perfect joy and elation I'd always imagined accompanying that second line were eerily absent. I was left with only confusion, disbelief, and fear.

I blinked back confused tears as my fingers fumbled for the phone and my shaking hands called the only person I could—my best friend. For the next several minutes, both of us sat in shock, alternating between phrases of amazement and disbelief with intermittent bouts of stunned silence. I resolved to see my doctor the next morning and spent the remaining hours of the night in restless shock, staring at the ceiling.

The following morning I walked into the doctor's office, steeled and ready to be strong, but the moment the words "I'm pregnant" escaped my lips, I found myself sobbing uncontrollably. The receptionist quietly whisked me to a back room, holding me as I cried and told her about my husband. The next thing I knew I was in a darkened room, a screen in front of me displaying a tiny baby... Jason's baby. As I watched in complete wonder, the flicker of light pulsed and the rapid drum of our baby's heart thumped. It was the single most beautiful sound I had ever heard.

I am a Christian. Though I've always gone to church, I never considered myself to have the closeness to God that I'd heard other Christians talk about. However, in the months before Jason died, I felt God's undeniable tug on me, drawing me closer to Him. Through that He presented passages of His Word that, little did I know, would help me through both the heartache and the joy of the events that lie ahead of me. In the weeks before Jason's death, I had been studying the book of Isaiah in the Bible, specifically Isaiah 61:1-4. In verses 2 and 3, the Lord promises "to comfort all who mourn and provide for those who grieve...to bestow upon them a crown of beauty instead of ashes." That day, as I watched my baby through bittersweet tears, those words finally resonated with me. Just then the ultrasound tech grabbed my shoulders and pulled me toward her. She embraced me tightly, and I felt her shoulders shake as her tears soaked my shirt. Through sobs she whispered the familiar passage, "beauty from ashes, sweet Jenny. Beauty from ashes."

I am continually amazed at the ways God has shown Himself through all of this. Through the heartache and the joy, He has taught me to trust completely in Him to carry me through. At times those lessons were subtle. In others they were blatant, violent, and shattering. Nonetheless, they were necessary. I still struggle with the anger, the sadness, and the questions that come with loss, but I find tremendous peace in knowing that even though I may not understand, God is in control, and all I need to do is trust Him.

Jason's little boy is due in early March. While it breaks my heart that his son will never know him, that he will never feel his tender hugs or receive his loving kisses, I find comfort and joy in knowing that Jason's legacy will live on through memories and stories. And I anxiously await the day that our friends, family, and I can share those precious memories with his son. Meanwhile, though the obstacle course of emotions I experience day by day is challenging, I feel overwhelmingly blessed for the comfort of beauty from ashes...words that are forever written on my heart.

Paperweight

fiction by

Barbara Gildea

A light snow was falling as Charlie Reardon left the diner and made his way down Madison Street. He looked at the long cold walk that led to his street and wondered how long he would he able to keep this up. Shivering in the cold, he stumbled from one streetlight to the next. His winter jacket—all that remained from his days repairing lines for the phone company—was unzipped, the waterproof exterior falling away to reveal a red flannel pattern.

It was Charlie's choice to do his drinking at the diner instead of the local bar. The bar was too far for his knees to manage the walk home in this weather and full of people he knew that wanted to talk. Talking was for front stoops, Charlie always said, and bars were for drinking. Or, in his case, diners.

River Falls was a small town and on a Tuesday night, most of the residents had put their kids to bed and were sneaking a glass of wine or a bottle of beer. Few were out on the streets besides the young hurrying home before curfew or the old, like Charlie, for whom time held less meaning.

Shortly after Charlie left the Dish Diner, Mr. Townsend, who owned the place, called the station. The sheriff sent a car, which was now slowly rolling down the street a hundred paces behind Charlie. Long experience had taught Officer Crawley that offering Charlie a ride would be met with vicious ridicule. Mr. Reardon was quite spry for his 78 years. Crawley would follow Charlie until he made it home.

With one hand wiping the light snow from his eyes, Charlie focused on reaching the mailbox. It wasn't that he was too drunk to handle the walk, it was that his knees were too old to handle his drink —or at least the problems of balance that came after five measly beers. He hadn't noticed the cop car yet. His thoughts were for his wife alone. He sighed and said to the mailbox, "Jean'll be up. Then I'll be in for it."

In that way, Charlie continued down the long street, willing movement into knees and focusing his next few steps. He took the third right off Madison onto the quiet dead end where his house sat bordering the woods. He could hear his keys jingling among the coins in his jacket pocket and was glad of the fancy inner hook that he tied them to. Jean had showed him what the hook was for back when the company had passed out the new uniform.

Reaching his house at last, Charlie grasped the railing to help himself up the few steps to the front door, whose red paint was in need of another coat. Jean had insisted that they paint the door red, believing that in their retirement they would need all the help they could get and it wouldn't do to start forgetting where they lived.

Officer Crawley observed that Charlie got his keys into the lock just fine and knew that he would be all right alone tonight. He idled just long enough to make sure Charlie remembered to close the door behind him, before slowly turning his car around and continuing back to the station.

At home, Charlie waited inside the door for angry words to come. Nothing. He struggled with his boots until they lay in the bin near the front door. He dropped his keys into the chipped white and blue porcelain bowl that Jean had purchased for that purpose. One hand trailed along the banister of the stairs that lead to the bedrooms and the other walked along the wall until he found the light. Switching it on, Charlie blinked in surprise. He hadn't realized it was so dark.

Charlie found his first surprise in the kitchen. On the granite countertops that were an anniversary gift to themselves lay a note propped up near a full glass of water and two aspirins. Not just any note. Charlie picked up the little origami bird and turned it around in his hand. She was improving. This bird's wings really moved. He popped the aspirin and washed it down with the water. It was Jean's way of forgiving his late night. She always talked about how people who kept birds in cages sorely misunderstood the thing.

Placing the glass in the sink, Charlie gazed up at Jean's hazy watercolor picture of the river that flowed behind the house. Jean enjoyed picking up a new hobby just as much as she liked abandoning one for another. At least the watercolor wasn't as noisy as the week she thought she might learn to play the tin whistle. Opening the fridge, Charlie looked for something that Jean wouldn't mind if he snacked on. It was easier to find that he thought. Next to a take-out container laid an origami arrow, pointing the way. Thank you, Jean.

Container in hand, Charlie headed into the living room and the late night TV that had become his habit in these recent months. He nodded a greeting at the fish on the wall, sadly not one he had caught himself, but one Jean had fished out of a yard sale years ago. He always released the fish he caught. But Charlie agreed with Jean that the fish looked good, hanging there against the wooden wall panels. Waiting for him on his side table, he found his third surprise: an origami box. He opened it to reveal the television clicker.

Chuckling, he thought about what a fine mood Jean must have been in that night. A fine mood indeed.

Two nights later, Cecelia Martin was having a rough evening at the diner, a condition not improved when Charlie Reardon walked through the door and sat at one of her tables.

Celia, as her friends called her, was balancing her night job waitressing tables at the Dish with her day job part-time in the local library. With Rick at the mill all hours of the day and still barely making enough to keep their family of four boys in sneakers and shorts, it was all she could do to manage the house as well. Four boys to get up, get showered, get out the door, get to school, get to sports, get fed, get homeworked and get to bed. On a day like today, when last night was spent nursing the youngest through a spot of a stomach virus, it was all she could do to stay on her feet.

And now Charlie was here. Could the day get any longer?

"Hello, Charlie," she said pulling out her pad and readying her pen. "What can I get for you today?"

"You know," Charlie said, peering up at her, "none of the others even bother asking."

"You know my thoughts there."

"I suppose I do." Charlie made a grand show of pulling out his menu and pursuing it.

"It appears, being Thursday, I'll have the meatloaf special and a light draft. Thank you kindly."

Pretending to write down every word, Celia replied, "Right on up."

Tucking her pad into her apron and her pen behind her ear, Celia caught the sidelong looks the other diners were giving her. As if she were giving Charlie a hard time. If they really cared about Charlie, they'd be doing exactly what Celia was doing, making sure to ask for every order and deliver the artery-clogging food and light draft after light draft only when asked. She understood it had been tough on Charlie when old Jean passed about six months ago, but the man should be learning to take care of himself, prepare proper food, and not end up in the Dish every night for a meal and a drink.

Calling out the order to Jim, the cook, Celia took a moment to step out of her shoes and flex her feet. The supporting arches the doctor prescribed were in no way as life-changing as the box claimed. She grabbed Charlie his beer and opened it with one quick twist, grabbing a glass and slipping back into her shoes. Her father was a drunk and Celia never forgot. It's one of the reasons why she fell for Rick, who was one of those men who could have three beers at a barbeque and just stop.

The night passed in an uncomfortable blur. There was a party from the local elementary school, fifteen kids sugared up on Strawberry Blast Supremes. A bowling team celebrated the league win with dinner and a few rounds of shots, going on about how they had more time to spare and more beer to strike, before they split. Eleanor, Alice and Nell, the last survivors of the town's founding members of the Daughters of the American Revolution, were apparently in a competition to see which one could send back the most food.

All the while, Charlie Reardon sat in his corner booth and put back his meatloaf, his pie and his beers.

Finally, the dinner crowd shuffled out and the late crew shuffled in. Celia had time to duck out the back for a quick phone call home to check in on her boys. Placing her phone back in her pocket as she stepped through the door, Celia realized her lingerers had left their tab on the table at last and all that remained to her was Charlie. Gathering the tip and calculating how close she was to that pair of expensive sneakers she knew Peter, her oldest, wanted for his birthday, she slipped into the booth across from Charlie.

"How's it going then?" Celia asked.

Charlie didn't answer right away, but gazed at her with bloodshot eyes. He picked up his bottle and peeled the label, making small triangles that he stacked on his placemat.

"You're very good, you know."

"Best darn waitress this town has ever seen."

"Not a waitress. A mom."

Celia looked again at Charlie. Red eyes, red nose. He didn't sound drunk. Still. "You should be finishing up now, Charlie. I bet I can get one of the busboys to give you a lift home. Still snowing tonight, even if it isn't sticking."

"Mean it." Charlie began to fold the placemat next. "You're a great mom. Got all the tells."

Curiosity got the better of her. "What's that, then?"

Charlie smiled. "I saw the way you ducked out just now, cell phone in hand. Bet that was a phone call home, right?" He paused, but after Celia's small nod, he rushed right back in. "And with all those kids, earlier. You had those crayons down and placemats flipped over in a jiffy, convincing them there was nothing better in the world than playing Pictionary, keeping them distracted and happy while their parents had a moment of peace. And now you're offering to get me a ride home?" Charlie took a slow pull from his beer. "Yep. A mom."

Celia wasn't sure if Charlie was making fun of her and she damn sure wasn't going to stay and find out. "I'll close out your tab."

Charlie stared down at the placemat he continued to fold as she rose, but before Celia turned to leave, he said, "They never come by anymore, you know."

Celia looked down at Charlie, who didn't meet her eyes. She held in a breath, thinking she should just walk away, cash out and be done with it, but Charlie wouldn't look. She slipped back into booth. "Who, Charlie?"

"The kids." Charlie's eyes were red when he raised them.

Celia was reminded of her boy, Ned. Ned didn't say much, but when he did, you listened. "Why's that, Charlie?"

"I don't know. Not since the day she died. She was at home, you know?"

Celia's voice was soft. "No, I didn't know that."

"I just had to take her home at the end." Charlie finished what remained in his beer.

"The kids did good, then. Lucy's local and got to see her mom every day, and Kevin made the drive when he could. Even Luke flew down. They were all here. And now they're gone. Just like that."

The tinkling of the door singled the arrival of more customers. Catching Daphne's eye, Celia signaled that she should take them. "You know there wasn't anything you could do, Charlie," she said. "Cancer like that, nothing you can do."

"I know. It's not that—" Charlie stopped and cleared his throat. His eyes flickered to the table and back into her eyes. "I know that. But why didn't the kids come back? Was it Jean all along for them? Their mother? Was there something else I should have done?"

Charlie stopped, his fingers folding, folding, folding the paper. Celia didn't think there was anything she could say. The diner was so quiet, she could hear the tick of the old clock with a smiling face that hung above the customers.

Charlie pushed the placemat toward her, a tightly folded green mass. His hands hovered above the folds, grabbing one and pulling.

"It hopped! My word," Celia said. "It's a frog."

"For your boy." Charlie reached into his pocket when Celia smiled down at the little frog she knew Ned would love. Charlie left the money on the table between them, standing up with care. He stood near the booth for a minute. "I'd just like to know that I did what I could. I don't know." Charlie pulled on his coat. "I guess you never know."

"I guess not."

The bells rang as Charlie walked out.

Celia sat at the table, holding the little frog and feeling how light it was. Such a joyful little creation. She had underestimated Charlie all this time. She was so lucky. Her boys were only a walk away, all tucked up inside her house, waiting for her, while Charlie made his long way home to an empty house. She stood and ran to the door, throwing her apron at Daphne, asking her for five more minutes.

Celia ran into the light snow and saw Charlie's receding form, barely a block away.

She sprinted after. "Charlie! Charlie."

One hand on the light post and the other grabbing for his back pocket, Charlie turned.

"Celia? What is it?"

"It's just, it's just—" Celia held up a hand while she took a few breaths. "I don't know much; my boys are still young, and it's all I can to keep them happy even when I can't buy them designer shoes, but I know this. I'm doing my job, but at some point, you have to let them go. They are their own people, you know? Little souls. They've got to make their own way."

They stood together as the snow fell softly around them. Charlie nodded. Charlie smiled. He patted her arm. "You're a good girl, Cecelia. Get on back in now. You've got no coat."

Celia nodded. She watched Charlie turn and struggle toward the mailbox. She thought about her boys in the future, all grown and scattered. Would she be enough to call them back?

The bells above the diner door rang when Celia stepped back in. She had a few quick words with Daphne and stuck her head into the office to tell Mr. Townsend to call the sheriff for Mr. Reardon's escort home. She changed. She didn't know that Mr. Townsend had just received the invoice for the new roof and didn't hear a word she said. She didn't know the cop car was never called. She didn't know about Mr. Reardon until the next day.

They found Charlie facedown in the river that meandered through the wood behind his street. Whether the red door had failed to stop him or the woods had called louder, no one would ever know.

The slow pool where his body had finally rested had frost covering its edge and snow was visible on its banks. Small pieces of brightly colored paper floated around him.

His kids came for the funeral. Celia saw them now, standing next to their father's coffin, shocked still and white faced. Dazed from sudden loss. As she watched, waiting in the line at the funeral home to pay her respects to Charlie, waiting a long time, she saw the clenched hands. The tears.

Celia had heard the stories of what Charlie's kids found when they finally went into their father's home. How the aspirin and water were waiting on the counter next to an origami boat, and the clicker was hidden inside a bushel of paper flowers. There was even a paper box in the fridge that held half of a sandwich.

The creations were on the television and under the sofa. There was one in the fish's mouth and another in the pot under the sink. They lined the stairs to the bedrooms, and were heaped on the front table next to a white and blue bowl that held odds and ends. Charlie must have been busy in those last few months, as no one who visited the house to say good-bye to Jean could recall a single one.

Kneeling in front of the waxy man that used to be Charlie, Celia said a silent prayer, wishing him well and telling him how much her boys loved that little green frog. Froggie had a place of honor on the kitchen counter and was more often in the hands of one of the boys.

Ned even insisted Froggie have his own place at the dinner table.

Shaking hands with Charlie's daughter, Celia told her how it was a real pleasure to be able to sit with him after a tough shift. "He even made me a little origami frog. My kids love it."

Lucy smiled through her tears. "You know, that origami was everywhere in the house, but there was one box of flowers apart from the rest, on Dad's nightstand in his bedroom. Some perfect flowers, some mangled ones. Mum's last hobby, I'd bet, abandoned in the end."

She paused. "Thank you. For coming. And the meatloaf. Dad loved the Dish meatloaf." Lucy reached for Celia's hand. "And for taking care of him. Especially for that."

Getting into the car to go home to her boys, Celia slipped out of the black heels that matched her one good dress. She decided to stop on the way home and pick up an origami beginner's kit. It was time to see if she and her boys could make Froggie a friend. All at once, it came to Celia that he might be a little lonely, sitting there all alone on the counter.

Queen And Knave
fiction by
Elizabeth Yon

The ship was a dying animal. Most of it had gone dark in the third week out of port, leaving him with only the command node and the linkage corridor unimpaired. The life support system wheezed like a stricken lung in the blackness of his cabin and in the tiny galley, and he had taken to sleeping in a hammock slung between bulwark struts in the engine room. It was dim there, too, but at least the operating lights of the machinery allowed him to move through the snug space without an emergency lantern. He found some comfort in the low throb of the engine, and in the almost biological smell of its oiled warmth. He held a barely conscious superstition that his presence in the engine room would prevent further, and more catastrophic, system failures.

His cargo was contraband. Nothing dangerous, just an intelligent library bound for some rich colonists. It was illegal, and probably stolen to boot, but it had seemed like an easy plum of a transport after the weapons run he'd squeaked through six months earlier. A plum, sure. He should never have agreed to pilot such a shitty excuse for a transport ship. Mere camouflage, the elegant export merchant had said. Her lips were scarlet delicacies, a black heart tattooed on the bow of the upper and the full, pouting curve of the lower. He'd always had a weakness for beautiful women. Why, she's sound as your own heart, she whispered. And he had nodded and rubbed his knuckles absently against the scar that twisted the flesh over that dubious organ, his ugly good-luck charm.

The cargo cell was different. State of the art and gleaming, it looked like a newly minted moon as it glided down the loading track toward the ship. Its linkage port was the size of a cathedral door, and it dwarfed the battered little transport.

Must be some library. He lit a cigarette and inhaled half of it in one breath. Nerves. He suffered from them more often lately, since his surgery. Since he'd become aware of the constant, fragile rhythm of his heartbeat, soft as a ticking bomb and as ominous.

The export merchant pursed her heart-patterned lips at him. Oh, it is. It is the only one of its kind, and worth more than your life. A tiny smile took some of the sting out of her words, but her eyes held none of the cultivated warmth of her voice. My client will expect it delivered on time and in perfect condition.

I'm a professional, honey. You got no worries. He had not been bragging. In twenty years of pirates and dogfights, junk ships and backstabbing clients, he had never lost a shipment. That was for amateurs and dead men, not for Jack Fairday. He had grinned roguishly at his pretty employer. *No worries. I'm a sure bet.*

Now, halfway into the three-month run, the ship sometimes shuddered and howled. The sound crawled inside his skull and bloomed there like an ink stain. In a crazy way, it reminded him of his grandfather's house on Earth, an ancient stone and timber structure that captured the wind in its high eaves and fashioned of it an angry voice. As a boy, he had listened to that growling wail from the dark island of his bed and pulled the blankets over his head in terror.

He could not find the source of the tremors or the awful sounds, though he ran diagnostic sweeps at regular intervals. He worried about the cargo, the library he was risking his neck to truck into the wasteland.

What's in it, he had asked, expecting to be told that it was a collection of banned pornography. He could not have been further from the mark.

Fairytales, the export merchant said. She was solemn, almost reverent, and he'd thought she was having him on, but she shivered instead of laughing. They are old and beautiful, but—well, just be very careful.

He was transporting kiddie stories, and hoping he lived through it. He had not slept much since the disturbances began, and he blamed his growing fatigue for the newest hellish wrinkle. He had begun to see ghosts.

In the linkage corridor, where the lights were still bright and the air scrubbers continued their sanitizing work, flecks of crimson lay scattered on the grey rubber matting like showered blood. He knelt and touched one with a cautious forefinger. It was soft and yielding, like silk and flesh. A rose petal. He carried it to his nose, but it had no scent, and it curled in his fingers and wafted mistily away. A shudder ran over the ship and over his own skin, raising goosebumps.

This cultivar's called The Queen of Hearts. Remember her, lad? The whisper was so faint he could have imagined it, but the rangy figure that shimmered at the end of the corridor was unmistakable. His grandfather had grown some magnificent roses, once upon a time in a land far, far away. The ghost raised a perfect bloom to its lips and blew. The petals unwound in a scarlet smoke that drifted toward him. When it dissipated, his grandfather was gone. A low growl emanated from the walls, and his heart rolled and thudded in his chest like shifting ballast. He crouched there, rubbing at the aching vine of his scar, and then he stood and made his way to the control node. The glowing blue lozenge of the life support indicator comforted him. His knees wobbled, and he sank into the pilot's chair and leaned back, staring out at the unending darkness. He was well outside the shipping lanes, gambling on the ship's soundness and saving himself the heavy tolls and tiresome boarding patrols. If he lost it out here, no one would find him for a very long time. He thought about the nature of luck.

His grandfather had loved cards. He almost never lost, no matter the game. That might have made things monotonous for his opponents, but the old man had told such clever stories during play that his winning seemed only fair in exchange. *Look at this card, Jack.* In the tarnished glass of memory, he watched as his grandfather's roughened fingers drew the Queen of Hearts and made her dance in front of his wide eyes. *She's a goddess, the ruler of worlds, and she loves a gambler.* The old man cast the card down with a practiced flick of his wrist. It sailed across the polished oak table and spun around so that the Queen's enigmatic gaze locked with his. From somewhere far away, he heard his grandfather's deep growl. *But she doesn't care for too great a show of luck, and she'll kill you if she can.* He remembered there were roses on the back of the card, blood red and lush in a black labyrinth of thorns.

From the linkage corridor, as though from a great distance but closing fast, came a throaty, desolate howl that iced his veins. His reverie was shattered and he leapt up, only to stagger as a series of muffled detonations erupted in the engine room beneath his feet. There was a sound like a winter gale from the corridor. The floor under his boots heaved and subsided. He endured a breathless moment of suspended panic, and then the ship's navigation functions shut down, lights winking out like snuffed candles across his workstation. A sinister quiet filled the space where the ship's delicate hum had been. The serene blue glow of the life support indicator faltered and went out. He was adrift.

He groped his way to the corridor hatch in the sickly green glare of the overhead emergency lantern. He had to crank open the door and he cursed and sweated as he wrestled with the stiff handle of the door jack. He managed a slit wide enough to slip through, and tumbled into the corridor. The light here was dim and grey, and he could see that the port to the cargo cell was wide open. He guessed that the lock failed when the systems crashed. He pulled himself up from his hands and knees and gazed down the corridor. Drifts of scarlet rose petals lay piled in the curve where the walls and floor met, and spilled out into the corridor in a tide of mangled silk. Without the scrubbers to remove it, their heavy perfume hung on the thinning air. The diffused light streamed from the cargo cell, as did a wintry smell like water and stone. He thought he might even detect a sharper, sweeter smell in this sudden banquet of scents. Pines, a forest of them. The cold, soft light resolved itself into snow. The first fat flakes drifted down in slow, lazy spirals and kissed his eyelashes. The fragrant air turned to lead in his lungs, and the corridor went dark.

She'll set her wolves on you, Jackie boy, if you're cocky. He heard his grandfather's rust and rumble voice close to his ear, and thought he could feel the whiskey warmth of it. He rolled onto his side, but did not open his eyes. He waited for the old man to say more, and only a cold wind touched his ear. An enormous crack like a lightning strike roused him, and he sat up in the gloom and the ghostly swirl of the blizzard that blew from the cargo cell. The overhead storage bins to starboard had burst open and spewed their contents over the snow and roses. He saw the duffel he carried when in port and crawled over to it, dragging it up his body as he reeled to his feet. His head thundered with the labored beat of his heart, and his lungs burned. He looked over his shoulder toward the airless control node.

Not that way, laddie, his grandfather chuckled in his smoker's voice. *Your luck's run out in that direction.*

He turned toward the cargo cell. The linkage port yawned like the entrance to a forgotten temple. Beyond it stretched the forest, dark and infinite. He did not understand how that could be, but the trees ran away from him in endless ranks. He could see the rough bronze scales of their trunks and the starched green of their needles. The snow filled the grey sky and dashed against the sketches of distant mountains. He lurched through the port and the sudden immensity of open air was real enough to fill his lungs and give him hope. All around him, sugared with snow and blooming more vigorously in spite of it, were the roses. They lay between the crooked toes of the trees and stretched in bright swaths where moss might have grown. Their fragrance was like wine, and he laughed and turned to look back toward the linkage corridor. It was gone, and only his boot prints slowly filling with white showed the way he had come.

I made it, Pops, he shouted. *Lucky Jack made it through again.* He waltzed drunkenly with the tattered duffel in his arms and trampled the carpet of roses.

227

His heart quivered in protest at all it had endured. Still grinning, he leaned against a tree and fumbled in his breast pocket for his cigarettes.

A whisper in the forest drew his attention. It was a sound so faint he could not be sure he had heard anything at all, and he stood straining his ears and looking wildly about. There it was again, like the softest pressing of the snow. The sudden crackle of a snapped twig set his heart aflame with adrenaline, and he swung toward the sound. The snow coalesced into a form at first familiar, upright and rangy. Then it sprinted toward him, streaming white and silver, falling forward as it came. Its powerful haunches and shoulders hurled it onward, true as an arrow. The red roses seemed gathered in its long jaws, the hot tongue panted to taste him. Its eyes were starless black. With a shout, he turned to flee, and the snow whirled dizzily around him and he fell. For a long time he fell until the frozen ground slammed up to meet him and the beast crashed down on him with its hard paws. His duffel flew from his hand, its contents showered forth, and the old well-thumbed deck burst its worn band and fanned across the snow. *Queen trumps Jack, laddie.* The gravelly chuckle turned to a snarl. Grim and lovely amid the fallen cards, the Queen of Hearts stared blindly up into the storm.

ABOUT WRITE ON EDGE

Where inspiration meets community.

Write on Edge (formerly The Red Dress Club) was created as a place for writers to gather, exchange ideas and learn something about the art of storytelling.

We welcome any and all writers, regardless of level – anyone interested in writing has a place here. We are also open to writers of all genres: Fiction or non-fiction. Fantasy, young adult, chick lit, memoir – there are no limits.

Even though we have changed our name, we still are inspired by a blog post by Jenny Lawson, The Bloggess, about a Red Dress.

For many of us, our Red Dress is our dream to become a published writer. Maybe we just need a little extra motivation.

Maybe we just have to try to Write on Edge.

Visit us online at
www.writeonedge.com

ABOUT BANNERWING BOOKS

Bannerwing Books is an independent publishing imprint based in central Massachusetts.

For more information, please visit them online at
www.bannerwingbooks.com